OREGON COAST

BEST PLACES®
DESTINATIONS

OREGON COAST

2ND EDITION
EDITED BY STEPHANIE IRVING

SASQUATCH BOOKS
SEATTLE

Printed in the United States of America.
Published in the United States by Sasquatch Books
Distributed in Canada by Raincoast Books
Second edition

Series editor: Kate Rogers
Assistant editor: Novella Carpenter
Copy editor: Christine Clifton-Thornton
Cover design: Nancy Gellos
Cover photo: J.H. Pete Carmichael/The Image Bank
Foldout map: Dave Berger
Interior design adaptation and composition: Fay Bartels, Kate Basart, and Millie Beard

ISSN: 1522-5461
ISBN: 1-57061-174-2

SASQUATCH BOOKS
615 Second Avenue
Seattle, WA 98104
(206)467-4300
books@SasquatchBooks.com
http://www.SasquatchBooks.com

Special Sales

BEST PLACES® guidebooks are available at special discounts on bulk purchases for corporate, club, or organization sales promotions, premiums, and gifts. Special editions, including personalized covers, excerpts of existing guides, and corporate imprints, can be created in large quantities for specific needs. For more information, contact your local bookseller or Special Sales, Best Places Guidebooks, 615 Second Avenue, Suite 260, Seattle, Washington 98104, (800)775-0817.

Sasquatch Books publishes high-quality adult nonfiction as well as children's books, all related to the Northwest (San Francisco to Alaska). For information about our books, contact us at the above address, or view our site on the World Wide Web.

CONTENTS

THE NORTHERN OREGON COAST

THE SOUTHERN OREGON COAST

ACKNOWLEDGMENTS

Oregon Coast covers the wild (and not-so-wild) Oregon Coast from A to, well, B (Astoria to Brookings). It couldn't have been done without the myriad reports from Best Places scouts with a big thanks to one in particular who literally eats, sleeps, and bikes the coast—Richard Fencsak. He knows just about any town on the coast as well as he knows his hometown at the mouth of the Columbia. Combine Fencsak's insider tips with the outdoor expertise of Terry Richard, author of *Inside/Out Oregon*, the thriftiness of Nancy Leson, editor of *Northwest Budget Traveler*, and the trustworthiness of me, editor of *Northwest Best Places*, and you've got yourself one heck of a guide to one heck of a destination—the Oregon Coast.

But behind every expert, there's usually a vital support crew. Here it included stalwart factchecker Kristin Ladwig, who took on this assignment with grace, diligence, and speed; editorial assistant Novella Carpenter, who heralded this (her first) book through the production stage; and most of all, managing editor extraordinaire Kate Rogers, who took it upon her slender self to fatten up the book—at the last minute—when it looked a tad lean.

Finally, thanks to all of you who have befriended Best Places over the past decade and a half. We wrote this book for you, dear adventurer with good taste. So go, enjoy, and don't forget to report back.

—Stephanie Irving

ABOUT BEST PLACES GUIDEBOOKS

Oregon Coast is part of the BEST PLACES® guidebook series, which means it's written by and for locals, who enjoy getting out and exploring the region. When making our recommendations, we seek out establishments of good quality and good value, places that are independently owned, run by lively individuals, touched with local history, or sparked by fun and interesting decor. Every place listed is recommended.

BEST PLACES® guidebooks, which have been published continuously since 1975, represent one of the most respected regional travel series in the country. Each guide is written completely independently: no advertisers, no sponsors, no favors. Our reviewers know their territory, work incognito, and seek out the very best a city or region has to offer. We provide tough, candid reports and describe the true strengths, foibles, and unique characteristics of each establishment listed.

Note: Readers are advised that the reviews in this edition are based on information available at press time and are subject to change. The editors welcome information conveyed by users of this book, as long as they have no financial connection with the establishment concerned. A report form is provided at the end of the book, and feedback is also welcome via email: books@SasquatchBooks.com.

HOW TO USE THIS BOOK

ACTIVITIES

Each town along the coast has a variety of activities and attractions from which to choose. For quick and easy reference, we've created basic symbols to represent them, with full details immediately following. Watch for these symbols:

 Arts and crafts, galleries

 Beaches, swimming, beachcombing, and water recreation

 Bicycling

 Entertainment: movies, theater, concerts, performing arts, and events

 Fishing (salt water and fresh)

 Food and drinks

 Kid friendly, family activities

 Lighthouses and historical sites

 Parks, wilderness areas, outdoor recreation, and picnics

 Seals and sea lions

 Shops: clothing, books, antiques, souvenirs

 Views, scenic driving tours, and other attractions

 Whale watching, bird watching, and other wildlife viewing

RECOMMENDED RESTAURANTS AND LODGINGS

At the end of each town section you'll find restaurants and lodgings recommended by our BEST PLACES® editors.

Rating System Establishments with stars have been rated on a scale of zero to four. Ratings are based on uniqueness, value, loyalty of local clientele, excellence of cooking, performance measured against goals, and professionalism of service. In addition, we've included recommended bargain lodgings—the best place for the best price. These are usually $65 or less for one night's lodging for two.

(*no stars*)	Worth knowing about, if nearby
☆	A good place
☆☆	Some wonderful qualities
☆☆☆	Distinguished, many outstanding features
☆☆☆☆	The very best in the region

View Watch for this symbol throughout the book, indicating those restaurants and lodgings that feature a coastal or water view.

Price Range When prices range between two categories (for example, moderate to expensive), the lower one is given. Call ahead to verify.

$$$	Expensive. Indicates a tab of more than $80 for dinner for two, including wine (but not tip), and more than $100 for one night's lodging for two.
$$	Moderate. Falls between expensive and inexpensive.
$	Inexpensive. Indicates a tab of less than $35 for dinner, and less than $75 for lodgings for two.

Email and Web Site Addresses With the understanding that more people are using email and the World Wide Web to access information and to plan trips, BEST PLACES® has included email and Web site addresses of establishments, where available. Please note that the World Wide Web is a fluid and evolving medium, and that Web pages are often "under construction" or, as with all time-sensitive information in a guidebook such as this, may be no longer valid.

Checks and Credit Cards Most establishments that accept checks also require a major credit card for identification. Credit cards are abbreviated in this book as follows: American Express (AE); Diners Club (DC); Discover (DIS); MasterCard (MC); Visa (V).

Directions Throughout the book, basic directions are provided with each restaurant and lodging. Call ahead, however, to confirm hours and location.

Bed and Breakfasts Many B&Bs have a two-night minimum-stay requirement during the peak season, and several do not welcome children. Ask about a B&B's policies before you make your reservation.

Smoking Most establishments along the Oregon Coast do not permit smoking inside, although some lodgings have rooms reserved for smokers. Call ahead to verify an establishment's smoking policy.

Pets Most establishments do not allow pets; call ahead to verify, however, as some budget places do.

Index All restaurants, lodgings, town names, and major tourist attractions are listed alphabetically at the back of the book.

Reader Reports At the end of the book is a report form. We receive hundreds of reports from readers suggesting new places or agreeing or disagreeing with our assessments. They greatly help in our evaluations. We encourage you to respond.

OREGON
COAST

NORTHERN OREGON COAST

The northern Oregon Coast epitomizes the eternal struggle between water and land. From Astoria to Waldport—from the mouth of the Columbia River to Cape Perpetua—this rugged coastline is embossed with a series of headlands holding out against Neptune's fury, separated intermittently by expanses of sand. Numerous rivers sever the Coast Range and, finally, widen into estuaries just before emptying into the blue Pacific.

Demonstrating considerable foresight, the state of Oregon has decreed public access to all beaches sacrosanct. Many stretches of coastline, still in pristine condition, are preserved as state parks. Between the parks, however, development persists. Astoria, the largest city on the north coast, has a relatively stable population of 10,000 inhabitants, but other areas—such as Seaside and the stretch between Lincoln City and Newport—are bulging with resort hotels and related tourist concessions. Thankfully, though, most coastal towns are still hamlets of just a few hundred people.

Fishing and logging no longer dominate the coastal economy; tourism is quickly encroaching. Realizing this, many of the residents—an eclectic mix of artists, retirees, upwardly mobile surfers, blue-collar types, and entrepreneurs seeking to escape city life—are seeking a consensus on the appropriate amount of development. There is little agreement, except on two counts: that the coast's population will continue to grow, and that it rains a lot—55 to 80 inches annually.

ASTORIA

Founded in 1811 by John Jacob Astor's fur-trading company, Astoria really dates to the mid-19th century, when it began to thrive as a cannery town and shipping center. By the turn of the century, Astoria boasted a rip-roaring, Sodom and Gomorrah–type waterfront, with brothels and bars galore and a reputation as shanghai central for unwary sailors. Salmon was king, and as many as 36 canneries operated on the lower Columbia. Now, there are none.

The first American settlement west of the Rockies, which features a world-class maritime museum and a hillside dotted with restored 19th-century-era Victorian homes, continues to sport a blue-collar image. Astoria's reverence for the past blends nicely with its working-class present. The town is home to an active commercial fishing fleet, and many people are still employed in the wood products industry. Oceangoing freighters and tankers ply the Columbia River—right past a bustling downtown waterfront—on their way between Portland and the Pacific. Espresso bars have become de rigueur, but unlike many other coastal communities, T-shirt shops have yet to replace core businesses here. Astoria hasn't stood still waiting for the tourists to arrive, but they're visiting in ever greater numbers, precisely because the town isn't just another glitzy tourist destination.

ACTIVITIES

City Walk. The best way to "do" Astoria is on foot. Begin at the base of 17th Street, adjacent to the maritime museum, and head west along the river. The 14th Street Pier allows views of working tugboats and the goings-on of the Columbia River Bar and River Pilots. (Astoria is the only city on the West Coast where you can observe pilots getting on and off oceangoing vessels.) Eight blocks away, at Sixth Street River Park, is a covered observation tower (always open) where you can view river commerce and watch sea lions and seals search for a free lunch.

Living History. Fort Clatsop National Memorial (6 miles southwest of Astoria off Hwy 101; (503)861-2471) re-creates Lewis and Clark's 1805–06 winter encampment. Besides the audiovisuals and exhibits at the visitors center, there are living history displays (strings of black-powder muskets, construction of dugout canoes) in the summer.

Take a Break. Pacific Rim (formerly Ricciardi Gallery) (108 10th St; (503)325-5450) displays the city's finest selection of regional art. This family-owned gallery is where the locals hang out to enjoy espresso, juices, desserts, homemade soup, salads and seafood, and a great selection of reading material. On sunny days, this is the choice sidewalk-table hangout. Other days you might stumble onto a jazz concert. "It's a playground for artists," says singer Kelley Shannon, who runs the gallery with her mom, Patricia Shannon.

Museums. The Columbia River Maritime Museum (1792 Marine Dr; (503)325-2323) features a Great Hall with restored small craft and a panoramic, balcony view of the Columbia River. Seven thematic galleries depict different aspects of the region's maritime heritage. The lightship *Columbia*, the last of its kind on the Pacific coast, is moored outside (take a self-guided tour). The Flavel House (8th and Duane Sts; (503)325-2563), named after a prominent 19th-century businessman and the founder of the first successful Columbia River Bar Pilots organization, is Astoria's finest example of ornate Queen Anne architecture. The Heritage Museum (1618 Exchange St; (503)325-2203) is a beautifully restored building that once housed the city hall and jail. Both museums are operated by the Clatsop County Historical Society and feature local historical displays.

Up the hillside from the waterfront is a treasure trove of Victorian residences. Head up 17th Street (it gets steep!); between Franklin and Jerome Avenues are myriad examples of 19th-century homes, restored to their former splendor.

Midday Break. In addition to the killer desserts (carrot cake and freshly baked cookies) at Peter Pan Market (712 Niagara; (503)325-2143), you can stack a sandwich with six different kinds of meat. Nearby Niagara Park offers the perfect outdoor eating venue. Josephson's Smokehouse (106 Marine Dr; (503)325-2190) prepares superb alder-smoked salmon, tuna, and sturgeon.

Farm Fresh. Astoria's best sources for fresh fruits and veggies are Columbia Fruit and Produce (598 Bond; (503)325-4045), a kind of an indoor farmers' market that occasionally offers local organic produce, and the Community Store (1389 Duane St; (503)325-0027), which features a selection of healthy and organic packaged munchies.

Theater Productions. After you've seen the Astoria Column and Fort Clatsop, chances are you'll head for the Astor Street Opry Company (894 Commercial; (503)325-6104), that every summer for the past two decades showcases *Shanghaied in Astoria*. Locals will tell you, however, that the River (230 West

Marine Dr; (503)325-7487) is the place to go for summertime (and beyond) entertainment. Part coffeehouse (they roast their own), part Columbia River Repertory Theater, here's where you'll find excellent (and sometimes experimental) works by Seattle and Portland talent working with community actors. They showcase five plays during the summer, and the rest of the year this is the place for poetry readings, live music, storytelling, and even an occasional live radio broadcast.

Annual Events. The Scandinavian Midsummer Fest—an annual celebration of the city's heritage—includes ethnic foods, dancing, and music. A great locally run festival, it's held in June at Astoria High School; keep your eyes open for it. Reputedly the oldest continuously operating water-related festival on the West Coast, the Astoria Regatta features boat races that include sailboat and dragon boat races (dragon boats are Chinese boats that resemble dragons), parades on land and water, music, and lots of additional hoopla. Held the second week in August on Pier 2 at the Port Docks; (503)325-2711.

Time Out. Sports-oriented Merry Time (995 Marine Dr; (503)325-5606) has a healthy selection of microbrews and the most TV sets in town. You can even bet on the ponies here. Cafe Uniontown (218 W Marine Drive; (503)325-8707) offers a comfortable setting and acoustic music (on most weekends).

Hiking. Astorians like to call the woods that wrap around the south and east sides of their town an "urban forest." You can access it at either end of the Cathedral Tree Trail, so named because it leads to a 300-year-old spruce, a remnant of coastal forests of the past. Pick up the well-marked trailhead at the Astoria Column parking lot, or off Irving Avenue at 29th Street.

Oregon Coast Bike Route. Beginning on the north with the crossing of the Astoria-Megler Bridge from Washington, this designated long-distance cycling route follows Hwy 101 south to the California border. The total length is 368 miles, although that varies depending on the number of side roads ridden. Through-cyclists are encouraged to ride north to south because they will get a boost from prevailing winds to help them climb the 16,000 feet of total elevation they will encounter along the way. Trips that cover 50 to 60 miles per day average six to eight days. Although logistically easier to complete than a coastal hiking trip, the Oregon Coast Bike Route is not without its inconveniences. Bikers don't have the problems finding drinking water and campsites that hikers do, but they will need a high tolerance for heavy commercial and recreation traffic as they make their way along Hwy 101 on its unmarked shoulder bikeway. Most drivers, however, are accustomed to seeing cyclists along the highway and go out of their way to be courteous. The Oregon Department of Transportation's Bicycle/Pedestrian Program publishes a free map of the Oregon Coast Bike Route; (503) 378-3432. September is considered the best month to cycle the Oregon Coast. Often dry and sunny, September also has less highway traffic than July and August. Cyclists beginning the trip from the north should check for the latest information with Bike and Beyond, 1089 Marine Dr, Astoria; (503) 325-2961.

The 166-step climb up the Astoria Column, atop Coxcomb Hill, presents a panoramic view that's particularly lovely at sunset. If the climb's too much for you, the parking area offers a nice view, too.

Fat-Tire Destinations. Off-road bicyclists will like Astoria's many trails, mostly unimproved, that crisscross its urban forest. A number of unmarked trails spill down onto Irving Avenue, east of 22nd Street. Or head for the Astoria Column and pedal the Cathedral Tree Trail (always yield to hikers). After a quarter-mile, you'll spot plenty of offshoot opportunities. Warrenton's Fort Stevens State Park provides both paved and unpaved trails and uncrowded roads. Stop in at Bikes and Beyond (1089 Marine Dr; (503)325-2961) for information and free Oregon Coast bike maps. Ask employees about their favorite on- and off-road biking routes.

Paddling Destinations. Canoeists and kayakers can put in at the Astoria Yacht Club (on Young's Bay, underneath the old Young's Bay Bridge), the Columbia River's East-end Mooring Basin (off Leif Erickson Dr, at the east end of Astoria), and the John Day boat ramp (off Hwy 30, 5 miles east of Astoria). The latter, which leads into the John Day River, is a local "'yakers" favorite and a gunkholer's paradise. It traverses under a railroad trestle and into a calm section of the Columbia dotted with islands that are populated by eagles, ospreys, and four-legged wildlife.

Fishing and Boating. When you're surrounded by water on three sides, you know there must be some fish out there. Angling from a boat is your best bet for Columbia River estuary or ocean fishing. A number of area charter-boat operators offer salmon-, sturgeon-, and bottom-fishing excursions, as well as specialty river and dinner cruises. A search for the right boat might begin at Tiki Charters (at Astoria's West-end Basin; (503)325-7818). Numerous rivers provide excellent opportunities for catching salmon, trout, and steelhead. Astoria fishing guru Bob Ellsberg recommends the Klaskanine River (east of Astoria, along Hwy 202) for seasonal salmon and steelhead angling, and Cullaby Lake (off Hwy 101, 11 miles south of Astoria) for bass and trout.

Eagles and Elk. Approximately 48 eagles feed and roost at the Twilight Eagle Sanctuary, 8 miles east of Astoria (off Hwy 30 on Burnside Rd). The Jewell Meadows Wildlife Area (26 miles east of town on Hwy 202; (503)755-2264), with its rolling meadows, is at times populated by hundreds of elk, including majestic bulls with enormous racks.

On the Beach. Fort Stevens State Park (off Hwy 101 and Ridge Rd, 10 miles northwest of Astoria; (503)861-1671) is a 3,760-acre outdoor wonderland of forest trails, beaches, running and biking paths, and a freshwater lake suitable for swimming and fishing. The largest state park campground west of the Rockies—and one of the few places to camp along the northern beaches—Fort Stevens has 253 tent campsites, 128 electrical sites, 213 RV sites with full utility hookups, and 9 yurts. (Several campsites and one yurt are accessible by the disabled and are located near barrier-free rest rooms.) When fully occupied, as is frequently the case on summer weekends, Fort Stevens can be jammed by a couple thousand overnight guests and an equal number of day visitors. The result can be a crowded, noisy campground, complete with barking dogs, screaming children, and wailing sirens as the park staff attempts to keep order. It's not pristine, but at least it puts lots of people close to miles of sandy Pacific Ocean beach. Camping reservations can be made by calling Reservations Northwest, (800)452-5687, and are strongly advised on summer weekends, although it's always possible to pick up a cancellation. In addition to all the camping space, Fort

Stevens has two swimming areas at freshwater Coffenbury Lake, 5 miles of hiking trails, 9 miles of bike trails, viewing platforms at the south jetty of the Columbia River, and the military legacy of the Fort Stevens Military Reservation, which guarded the mouth of the Columbia from the Civil War through World War II and became part of the state park in 1976. The remnants of the *Peter Iredale*, an English sailing ship that ran aground during a storm in 1906, is a signature landmark in the park at the main day-use beach access area. Motor vehicles are allowed on the beach year-round south of the *Peter Iredale* to the town of Gearhart. Within the park you'll also find good razor clamming, choice windsurfing (in the ocean off the south jetty, or in nearby Trestle Bay), and productive surf fishing (particularly from the jetty; no license required, except for salmon).

The Oregon Coast Trail is a 350-mile route that closely follows the coastline from the Columbia River to the California border; however, lack of fresh water and frequent detours to highways make it a less than ideal backpack experience. Best to hike select sections.

Clam Digging. Digging for razor clams is usually good in Clatsop County, especially on the lowest-tide beaches of Fort Stevens State Park. Season runs from September through July 15 (but can be closed other times, so check with park officials). Bag limit is 24 clams daily. Many gas stations along Hwy 101 rent shovels; license unnecessary.

Views. The South Jetty lookout tower in Fort Stevens State Park is perched at Oregon's northwesternmost point, providing a supreme storm- and whale-watching spot. It also marks the start of the Oregon Coast Trail, which traverses sandy beaches and forested headlands all the way to the California border. The Lewis and Clark Interpretive Center—just across the river at Fort Canby in Ilwaco, Washington—provides the perfect vantage point for viewing the notorious Columbia River bar. In winter, Mother Nature struts her stuff as 15- to 30-foot swells, looking like an invading tidal-wave army, march over the bar into the river.

Logging Culture. It's way out of town, but Camp 18 (US Hwy 26 at milepost 18; (503)755-1818) is a combination loggers' theme park and chowhounds' fantasy. The decor: long, imposing tables sit beneath a towering, open-beamed ceiling; chain saws, hand tools, and logging photos line the walls. The interest quotient of the logging apparatus outside is, alone, worth a visit. Portions are huge and lean heavily toward meat 'n' potatoes. One piece of advice: Don't sass your waitress.

RESTAURANTS

COLUMBIAN CAFE ★★

The more publicity the Columbian gets (and it gets plenty), the more crowded it becomes. But this small, vegetarian-oriented cafe continues to be Astoria's best bet for good grub. The wait can still be long, but the interior has been redone and is considerably less cramped. From salmon chowder to vegetable bisque, the soups are satisfying and come with hearty slabs of grill-toasted garlic bread. The seafood and pasta dinners—sturgeon piccata, grilled halibut bathed in Thai nut sauce, rock shrimp spiked with cilantro and black beans—are perhaps the finest on the Oregon Coast. If you're feeling frisky, order the Chef's Mercy, a surprise potpourri of the day's best (and freshest) ingredients. Every Thursday evening in summer, the cafe features a sidewalk fish barbecue showcasing locally caught salmon, sturgeon, and tuna, which means Friday's menu often features something fun from the leftover fish. *1114 Marine Dr (at 11th St, next to the movie theater), Astoria, OR 97103; (503)325-2233; $; beer and wine; no credit cards; checks OK; breakfast, lunch Mon–Sat, dinner Wed–Sat.*

CANNERY CAFE ★

 Even if you're not hungry, drop by this airy, attractive waterfront cafe specializing in scrumptious baked goods, lunch fare, and a bevy of dinner choices (and chowder, of course). The building sits on pilings right over the water, and the Columbia River panoramas are superb—every table a stone's throw from the ship traffic and a plethora of finny, furry, and feathery critters. The sandwich selections include a turkey meatloaf and a panini du jour built around thick focaccia slices, while salads are colorful and creative (look for the black bean gazpacho salad, a thick, stewlike concoction). Sunday brunch (not your traditional buffet style) is the best in town, with such unusual choices as a mushroom roulade and pan-fried Dungeness crab cakes. *1 6th St (foot of 6th St), Astoria, OR 97103; (503)325-8642; $$; full bar; MC, V; checks OK; lunch, dinner Tues–Sun.*

RIO CAFE   ☆

The Mexican-food pipeline has finally reached Astoria, but instead of the usual Tex-Mex fare, this gaily decorated cantina offers inspired south-of-the-border cuisine. Three snappy salsas are a perfect match for the huge, handcrafted, crisp chips called *totopos*. And the Pescado Rojo—fresh sole or cod—is lightly breaded and grilled with a hot-and-sassy red chile and garlic sauce. *125 9th St (a block from the Columbia River), Astoria, OR 97103; (503)325-2409; $; beer and wine; MC, V; checks OK; lunch Mon–Sat, dinner Thurs–Sat.*

Favorite Oregon Coast restaurants: three cafes—the Columbian in Astoria, Midtown in Cannon Beach, and Blue Sky in Manzanita.
—Mary Blake, director of Seaside's Sunset Empire Park and Recreation District

LODGINGS

ROSEBRIAR HOTEL   ☆ ☆

 At the turn of the century, the Rosebriar was a private residence. Next it became a convent, and then a halfway house for the mentally disabled. Now, in its finest reincarnation, the place is a rambling 11-room inn. Guest rooms, though generally small, are beautifully furnished and have private baths. A full breakfast is included in the reasonable rates (which begin at $69). The common rooms are spacious and homey, while the outside grounds provide a gardenlike setting, including a porch and front-yard benches affording Columbia River views. All this is within easy walking distance of downtown. *636 14th St (at Franklin), Astoria, OR 97103; (503)325-7427 or (800)487-0224; $; MC, V; checks OK.*

COLUMBIA RIVER INN   ☆

 Astoria has more bed and breakfasts than any other town on the coast, so it's often difficult to pick the best here; we suggest this restored turn-of-the-century Victorian, painted a lovely blue with red and yellow trim, that offers four guest rooms (all with private baths), spacious living and dining areas, and elegant furnishings. The honeymoon room features a fireplace, canopy bed, and Jacuzzi. Gracious hostess Karen Nelson serves a full breakfast with just the right amount of conversation. Outside, amid a neighborhood brimming with Victorian residences, there's a terraced garden with a gazebo, benches, and Columbia River vistas. *1681 Franklin Ave (corner of 17th), Astoria, OR 97103; (503)325-5044 or (800)953-5044; $$; MC, V; checks OK.*

CLEMENTINE'S BED AND BREAKFAST

Astoria enjoys the Oregon Coast's largest collection of B&Bs, and this 1888 Italianate Victorian situated at the edge of downtown is a superb choice. Your enthusiastic and multitalented hosts, Judith and Cliff Taylor, offer a wealth of knowledge about north coast happenings (she's a master gardener and a cooking instructor; he knows his way around a kayak). Five nicely decorated rooms reflect the Taylors' attention to detail; breakfast reflects their ability to satisfy hungry guests. All the rooms have private baths and nice beds, and are appointed with fresh flowers from the garden. A second-floor suite features a gas fireplace and sleeps up to four guests. There's a cottage-style house next door that six or so can rent. *847 Exchange St, Astoria, OR 97103; (503)325-2005 or (800)521-6801; $$; AE, MC, V; checks OK.*

CREST MOTEL

 With 40 rooms sited on a forested bluff overlooking the Columbia River on Astoria's east edge, the Crest offers the best motel view in town. When it's foggy, the foghorns bellow up the hillside from the ship traffic below. In the large backyard, you can recline in lawn chairs and enjoy a bird's-eye view of the in- and outgoing tankers and freighters, or unwind in a gazebo-enclosed whirlpool. Pets are welcome; so is smoking in one section. All in all, this is the best alternative in town to B&B lodging. *5366 Leif Erickson Dr (2 miles east of downtown), Astoria, OR 97103; (503)325-3141; $$; AE, DC, DIS, MC, V; no checks.*

FRANKLIN STREET STATION

This is one of Astoria's oldest B&Bs, with a less-than-stellar location two blocks from downtown on a rather ordinary street lacking greenery. But the house itself has style and elegance. The interior is exquisitely appointed with Victorian furnishings, while frilly drapes frame the windows. There are six guest rooms; two look out to the river and have their own decks. An attic room, the Captain's Quarters, has the best view and its own living room. Unfortunately, the Italian owners do not live on-site and, therefore, are not always available; however, fine Italian coffees and cookies make up for any absences. *1140 Franklin St (between 11th and 12th), Astoria, OR 97103; (503)325-4314 or (800)448-1098; $$; AE, MC, V; checks OK.*

GRANDVIEW BED AND BREAKFAST

 The view is indeed grand from this rambling Victorian structure situated on an oversize, forestlike lot a few blocks from downtown. The former home of a cannery owner, the Grandview features a tower with an open balcony, a turret, lots of bay windows, and 10 guest rooms. Anastasia's Room—cozy, pastel-colored quarters with a queen bed and shared bath—is a steal. Rooms with a shared bath are discounted. All guests receive a continental breakfast with fresh fruit and juices; bagels, lox, and cream cheese; and homemade muffins. In winter, ask about "second night free" specials. *1574 Grand Ave, Astoria, OR 97103; (503)325-0000; $; DIS, MC, V; no checks.*

Gearhart has a Martha's Vineyard look, with a wide, white-sand beach backed by lovely dunes partially covered with bunch-grass. Razor clamming is popular.

GEARHART

Mostly residential, Gearhart exemplifies Oregon Coast architecture, with an assortment of beachfront, weathered-wood homes in shades of white and gray. Some of the dwellings are substantial, built by fashionable Portlanders when the coast was being discovered. Gearhart now showcases an interesting blend of well-to-do weekenders and local fishermen, artists, and retirees.

ACTIVITIES

The dunes at the end of Pacific Way are the perfect place to watch a sunset. There's even a bench and a gently sloping trail to the beach.

Tee Time. Gearhart Golf Course, west of Hwy 101, (503)738-3538, opened in 1892, is the second-oldest course in the West—a 6,089-yard layout with sandy soil that dries quickly; open to the public.

RESTAURANTS

PACIFIC WAY BAKERY AND CAFE ☆☆

Don't miss A Great Shop (576 Pacific Way; (503)738-3540), which features unusual but functional knick-knacks, from children's toys to books to fancy soaps and such.

This airy cafe, with hardwood floors, lots of windows, hip service, cool sounds, and plenty of espresso, is the only restaurant in downtown (such as it is) Gearhart. It continues to thrive on a mix of suspender-and-clam-shovel locals and out-of-town "gearheads"—the BMW-and-summer-beachfront-home crowd who comes to hang out, hobnob, and sample the best pastries and breads on the northern Oregon Coast. Breakfast is strictly continental-style, and the Greek sandwich and curried chicken salad are savory lunch possibilities. Crunchy-crust pizzas—available with unorthodox toppings (apple-chicken sausage or dill-ricotta pesto, for instance) if you prefer—and nightly specials, such as flank steak with garlic-mashed potatoes, fiery-hot curry, and cioppino, round out the appealing menu. Save room for baker Lisa Allen's luscious lemon meringue pie or whatever sweet thing she happens to be dreaming up, and pick up a loaf of the coast's best baguette on your way out. *601 Pacific Way (downtown, corner of Cottage), Gearhart, OR 97138; (503)738-0245; $$; beer and wine; MC, V; checks OK; breakfast, lunch, dinner Wed–Sun.*

LODGINGS

GEARHART OCEAN INN

With a New England–style architecture and a quiet, homey feel, these 11 attached cottages on the edge of downtown are low-cost charmers. All units are nonsmoking, and most (except 3, 4, 5, and 6) come with kitchens; some are suites with separate bedrooms, suitable for families. The interiors are appointed with beachy wicker furniture, throw rugs, and colorful comforters. Unit 11 is the biggest, with two bedrooms (sleeps as many as seven). *67 N Cottage (across from the Pacific Way Cafe), Gearhart; (503)738-7373; PO Box 2161, Gearhart, OR 97138; $; MC, V; checks OK.*

One of the coziest indoor locales around is the lounge of Gearhart's Oceanside Restaurant (1200 N Marion; (503)738-7789). The oceanfront setting overlooks a less crowded stretch of dunes and beach. The view is spectacular, especially at night, with white-capped waves breaking against a moonlit sky.

Above the Persian rugs, and over the European antiques, you'll find some excellent works from local Northwest artists at The Sand Dollar Gallery (Sand Dollar Square on Broadway; (503)227-6650).

SEASIDE

One hundred years ago, affluent beachgoers rode Columbia River steamers to Astoria from Portland, then hopped a stage-coach to Seaside, the Oregon Coast's first resort town. It seems the place has become more crowded every year since. On any summer weekend, the traffic lines up for a long way on Highway 101 and at the intersection of Broadway and Holladay, the town's main thoroughfares. The crowds mill along Broadway, eyeing the entertainment parlors, the sweet-treat concessions, and the bumper cars, then emerge at the Prom, the 2-mile-long cement "boardwalk" that's ideal for strolling (but watch out for skate-boarders, in-line skaters, and bicyclists).

ACTIVITIES

Live Music. Quatat Marine Park, which parallels the Neca-nicum River, is the setting for many free events. There are concerts every Saturday afternoon in summer—everything from folk to jazz to rock—all part of the "Where the Stars Play" music series sponsored by the Sunset Empire Park and Recreation District; (503)738-3311.

Secret Beaches. Ecola State Park, a gem of the Oregon parks system, has outstanding views, pocket beaches, and an extensive trail system within its 1,310 acres. The park caps a headland between Seaside and Cannon Beach and is famous around the world for the stunning photographs that are taken there. Views include those of Tillamook Rock, a mile off-shore with an inactive lighthouse perched atop its steep cliffs (the former light station was built offshore more than 100 years ago and abandoned in 1957; today it's a columbarium named "Eternity at Sea"). There is a hiker's camp 1½ mile north of the road end at the Indian Beach picnic area. The trail from the camp continues north over Tillamook Head and comes out in Seaside.

Hiking. The rugged 7-mile hike over Tillamook Head, part of Ecola State Park, is one of the coast's most rewarding for spectacular vistas, including a view of the Tillamook Rock Light-house. Part of the Oregon Coast Trail, this trail begins at the south end of Seaside and climbs 900 feet over Tillamook Head before joining the trail system in Ecola State Park north of Cannon Beach. The trail's northern terminus is at the end of Sunset Blvd in Seaside and its southern end is at the end of the road in Ecola State Park. The trail offers occasional ocean views, but the forest is often too thick to see much more than what lies immediately ahead. Clark's Viewpoint at 3.7 miles south of Seaside is thought to be the southernmost point of exploration by the Lewis and Clark expedition.

The Turnaround, on the Prom (at the western end of Broadway), is a great place to watch the sunset—and other people watching the sunset.

Another strenuous but sensational hike begins 14 miles east at Saddle Mountain State Park, off Hwy 26. A narrow, winding road leads to the trailhead, which proceeds 2½ miles—at times steep and gravelly—to the 3,283-foot summit. On a clear day, the ocean, the Columbia River, the Coast Range, and even Mount St. Helens are visible. Klootchy Creek Park (along Hwy 26, 2 miles east of the Cannon Beach junction) claims the world's largest Sitka spruce, and provides an opportunity to access the Necanicum River. There's a favored fishing hole right under the bridge.

Fishing. Local author and outdoorsman Bob Ellsberg calls the Necanicum River the north coast's best year-round fishing stream. Salmon, steelhead, and trout are all routinely pulled out of this swift-moving waterway, and access is very good. You can fish off of, or just below, the Avenue U bridge (adjacent to Hwy 101 on the south side of town). Follow Avenue U 4 blocks west to the ocean for razor clamming or surf fishing.

Surfing. The Point (along Sunset Blvd) offers the finest left-handed surfing waves in Oregon. A rock-strewn beach, radical riptides, and an overprotective contingent of locals limit water time for all but the experienced. Just a half mile north, the Seaside Cove offers a more forgiving wave, although the rocks are still plentiful. Cleanline Surf Company (719 1st Ave; (503)738-7888) is a great source for ocean-play equipment (surfboards and wet suits) and info. Oceangoing kayakers also frequent the cove (along Sunset Blvd), whose waters are approachable via an adjacent sandy beach.

Wildlife. Ecola State Park is another of Oregon's 29 designated whale-watching sites. The park's headlands provide a good perch for watching for the mammals. The system of islands that makes up Oregon's federal coastal wildlife refuge begins offshore at Ecola; birds sighted here include common murre, American black oystercatcher, rhinoceros auklet, and tufted puffin. Tide pools, rare along the northern coast's beaches, are also found here.

RESTAURANTS

BREAKERS ☆

Part of a large ocean-front motel complex, this place is far from an afterthought, even though it occupies a windowless basement location. An attractive seashore motif—sand-castle sculptures, colorful kites, and beach umbrellas—substitutes for ocean views. Seafood choices include a pearly white halibut fillet kissed with lime-cilantro butter, salmon simply braised in white wine, and sautéed Dungeness crab legs. And you'll have no beef with the way the kitchen prepares its New York and rib-eye steaks, which are marinated in herbs and balsamic vinegar and then broiled to order. Sunday brunch is a winner. *414 N Prom (part of the Ocean View Resort), Seaside, OR 97138; (503)738-3334 or (800)234-8439; $$; full bar; AE, DC, DIS, MC, V; checks OK; brunch Sun, dinner every day.*

DOOGER'S

As the line outside all summer will attest, this place is popular. Inside, it's a clean, smokeless, unkitschy, family place with friendly service. Stick with the simpler offerings, like the mighty fine chowder, the halibut, scallops, or the 2-pound bucket of steamers. Most fish can be prepared a number of ways. The Dooger's empire includes a larger version in Cannon Beach at 1371 S Hemlock, (503)436-2225; another at 900 S Pacific in Long Beach, Washington, (360)642-4224; and (as we go to press) one to come on the Astoria waterfront at the foot of Fifth Street. *505 Broadway (at Franklin), Seaside, OR 97138; (503)738-3773; $$; beer and wine; MC, V; local checks only; lunch, dinner every day.*

PREMIER PASTA

Buy pasta by the bag or the plate at this noodle joint on the Necanicum River. A dozen herbed varieties—from basil garlic and lemon-dill fettuccine to myriad tortellini—are yours for the asking. Order the linguine with clams or a garlic lover's sauce, or opt for the tricolored pasta—a blend of egg, spinach, and tomato-basil noodles finished with pesto. There's also chicken marinara, feta-olive lasagne, and an Italian version of the muffuletta sandwich, an enormous concoction oozing mozzarella and layered with salami and marinated veggies—for here or ready to go. The owners are big *Seinfeld* fans; ask them about the painting of Kramer hanging in the dining room. *1530 S Holladay Dr, Seaside, OR 97138; (503)738-3692; $; beer and wine; MC, V; local checks only; lunch Mon–Fri; dinner every day.*

THE STAND

Small, tidy, and austerely decorated—with 10 tables, and meals served in paper baskets with plastic forks—the Stand serves some seriously satisfying Tex-Mex chow. The place is patronized by a young skate-surf crowd, who appreciate the low prices and no-hassle service. You'll like the fresh—every day—corn tortillas and salsas. Not to mention the many burrito options, including a potent chile verde version packed with pork, Jack cheese, and a tango of green salsa. Veggie burritos and quesadillas are plump with zucchini, mushrooms, myriad peppers, cheese, and all manner of goodies. Our advice? When you're hungry, take to The Stand. *220 Ave U (1 block from the beach), Seaside, OR 97138; (503)738-6592; $; no alcohol; no credit cards; checks OK; lunch, dinner Mon–Sat.*

VISTA SEA CAFE

It may be frenzied outside at Seaside's busiest intersection, but inside Vista Sea Cafe you'll find a pleasant respite from the crowds. The meatloaf sandwich, Greek pasta salad, spanakopita, and lasagna are top-notch choices. Hefty pizzas piled high with toppings such as pancetta, Italian sausage, and Oregon blue cheese are the house

Cafe Espresso (600 Broadway; (503)738-6169) is the best spot in Seaside for joe-to-go, or try Bagels by the Sea (575 S Roosevelt Drive, Seaside; (503)717-9145) for traditional boiled-and-baked orbs.

speciality. *150 Broadway (on the corner of Broadway and Columbia), Seaside, OR 97138; (503)738-8108; $; beer and wine; AMEX, D, MC, V; checks OK; lunch, dinner every day (closed Wed–Thurs in winter).*

LODGINGS

ANDERSON'S BOARDING HOUSE ☆

Fir tongue-and-groove walls, beamed ceilings, and wood paneling recall traditional boardinghouse decor at this solid, turn-of-the-century, blue Victorian. There's even a working Victrola in the parlor. The house fronts Seaside's busy Holladay Drive, but the backyard slopes gently to the Necanicum River—convenient and close to the beach. All six guest rooms have private baths and a wicker-and-wood beachy feeling. There's also a riverfront, miniature Victorian cottage (with a full kitchen) that sleeps up to six people. Full breakfasts are included. *208 N Holladay Dr (at 3rd), Seaside, OR 97138; (503)738-9055 or (800)995-4013; $$; MC, V; checks OK.*

GILBERT INN ☆

Built in 1892, this Queen Anne–style Victorian located a block off the Prom presents a refreshing visual antidote to the nearby high-rises, espresso concessions, and surrey rentals. There are 10 guest rooms within the sprawling, light-yellow structure, all with period furnishings (as well as color TVs and phones), private baths, and a full breakfast. Richly finished tongue-and-groove fir covers the walls and ceilings throughout the inn, and a large fireplace highlights the downstairs parlor, decorated with lush green carpeting and cushy couches. The second-floor Turret Room shows off an ocean view and a four-poster bed, while the Garret, a third-story suite with brass beds (one queen, two twins), is great for families. *341 Beach Dr (1 block off the Prom), Seaside, OR 97138; (503)738-9770 or (800)410-9770; $$; AE, DIS, MC, V; checks OK.*

RIVERSIDE INN BED AND BREAKFAST

The Riverside continues to be Seaside's best bargain for traditional-style lodging. The 11 adjacent cottages are comfortable, spacious, and clean. While the front faces bustling Holladay Drive, the rear recedes gracefully to the Necanicum River. A large riverfront deck provides opportunities for fishing, semi-secluded sunbathing, or relaxing. The full breakfasts are top-notch, and the beach is just a few blocks away. *430 S Holladay Dr, Seaside, OR 97138; (503)738-8254 or (800)826-6151; $; AE, DC, DIS, MC, V; checks OK.*

SEASIDE INTERNATIONAL HOSTEL

A reconverted motel, this European-style hostel features traditional dormitorylike sleeping quarters (45 beds), shared bathroom facilities, and a large, well-equipped communal kitchen. There's an in-house espresso bar and outside decks, and the Necanicum River flows past the backyard. In the summer you can expect to meet travelers from all over the world, and intermingling is encouraged. Unlike traditional hostels, you don't have to leave during the day (the place remains open), and no curfew is imposed. Dorm rates are $14 for American Youth Hostel members ($17 for nonmembers). Private rooms with baths and TVs are available, and though they cost considerably more, they're still a veritable steal. *930 N Holladay Dr, Seaside, OR 97138; (503)738-7911; $; MC, V; no checks.*

SHILO INN

 We're wary of glitzy establishments that hog the shoreline, but this one has a good reputation. The setting is superb, the lobby is stylish and mirrored, and the prices are stratospheric. But all of the amenities expected in a resort hotel are here: indoor pool, steam room, sauna, workout room, and therapy pool. The choicest rooms face the ocean and are further graced with fireplaces, kitchens, and private patios. The Shilo frequently hosts conventions, so it's not the place to get away from the hubbub of urban life. The restaurant is spendy and not

Camping is allowed on Oregon beaches except within the city limits of Seaside, Cannon Beach, Manzanita, Rockaway Beach, Lincoln City, Newport, Bandon, and Gold Beach.

your best choice in town, but the dining room and the adjacent piano bar enjoy a gorgeous view. *30 N Prom (N Prom and Broadway at Seaside's turnaround), Seaside, OR 97138; (503)738-9571 or (800)222-2244; $$$; AE, DC, MC, V; checks OK.*

CANNON BEACH

Cannon Beach is an artsy community with a hip, upscale ambience and a love/hate relationship with the ever-increasing tourist hordes that converge on the town year-round, mainly because there's a lot to like. Strict building codes ensure that only aesthetically pleasing structures are built (usually of cedar and weathered wood). Galleries, crafts shops, and espresso parlors line either side of Hemlock Street, where meandering visitors rub shoulders with the coastal intelligentsia. The main draw continues to be the wide, inviting beach, which, fortunately, remains unchanged and among the prettiest anywhere.

ACTIVITIES

Beach Walks. Haystack Rock, one of the world's largest coastal monoliths, dominates the long, sandy stretch. At low tide you can observe rich marine life in the tidal pools, or take a 5-mile beach walk to Arch Cape (always consult a tide table beforehand). If you didn't attempt the trail over Tillamook Head from Seaside, try it from the north end of Cannon Beach. You can pick it up at a number of places within Ecola State Park—which also offers fabulous views and quiet picnic areas.

Hemlock Art Walk. Galleries abound in the Cannon Beach area, all on Hemlock Street, the main drag. Three especially good ones are the White Bird (251 N Hemlock; (503)436-2681), which features a variety of arts and crafts; the Haystack Gallery (183 N Hemlock; (503)436-2547), with a wide range of prints and photography; and Jeffrey Hull Watercolors (in Sandpiper Square, 178 N Hemlock; (503)436-2600), a collection of delicately brushed seascapes. The Cannon Beach Arts Association Gallery (1064 N Hemlock; (503)436-0744) features local artists.

Baked Goods. Sweet treats, and a loaf of bread that resembles the famous Haystack Rock are sold hot out of one of the few remaining brick, oil-fired hearth ovens on the West Coast at the Cannon Beach Bakery (144 N Hemlock; (503)436-2592). You can take out the soft inner part of the bread and put salsa or chili in the crust and use it as a unusual bowl. Hane's

"I was born and raised in the Bay Area. I owned a library services business in the heart of San Francisco's Financial District. The first time I came to Oregon I felt like I'd come home. After that, it never occurred to me to live anywhere else. I stand on the beach here and in one direction is the beautiful forest, in another the beautiful ocean. And even after five years, that beauty hasn't lessened." —Sally Wies, employee at the Cannon Beach Book Company

Bakerie (1064 N Hemlock; (503)436-0120) offers intricate fruit and cheese croissants and the town's best breads.

Books and Art. A good browse can be had at the Cannon Beach Book Company (132 N Hemlock; (503)436-1301). Or stop by the new Pacific Rim Gallery (131 W 2nd; (503)436-1253) for a peek at some fine regional art, jewelry, and cards. It's a branch of their original gallery in Astoria, with all the same artistic talent—but, alas, no espresso or music.

Beachside Spots. At Wayfarer (on the beach at Ocean and Gower, adjacent to the Surfsand Resort; (503)436-1108), the food's nothing to brag about, but the beachfront setting and the views of Haystack Rock and the Pacific can't be beat. In downtown, head for Bill's Tavern (188 N Hemlock; (503)436-2202), the hot spot for a brew.

Biking. When the sun comes out, three-wheelers are popular on the beach, mountain bikes on logging roads and trails. You can rent either at Mike's Bike Shop (248 N Spruce; (503)436-1266), which has been in business for over 25 years. Inquire here about favorite routes.

Fishing. Turn your back on the ocean—some of the best steelhead and trout fishing can be had in tiny Elk Creek, which merges with the Pacific just west of downtown. Good trout holes can be found by hiking upcreek, on the east side of Hwy 101.

Riding the Waves. The Northwest is not exactly a surfer's destination—but hang 10 here and you might find yourself with a big, wet grin. Surfers favor the "Needles" beachbreak, just south of Haystack Rock, and the right-handed waves at Indian Beach, within Ecola State Park.

Dig It. June's Sandcastle Day, a contest that draws sand sculptors from throughout the Northwest and Canada, has become Cannon Beach's busiest day. The crowds, and the traffic, are horrendous. If you visit during Sandcastle Day, get here early, and don't even consider driving or parking downtown. Leave your vehicle at the Tolovana Wayside (off S Hemlock, in Tolovana Park) and walk the beach into town. Be sure to reserve lodging well in advance. For information, contact the Cannon Beach Chamber of Commerce, (503)436-2623.

Quote on the wall of the Cannon Beach Book Company: "Wear the old coat and buy the new book."

RESTAURANTS

CAFE DE LA MER ★★

This post-'60s coffeehouse, which became Cannon Beach's first fine-dining establishment 20 years ago, has won a considerable following. The atmosphere inside is warm, and the food is conscientiously served and lovingly purveyed by owners Pat Noonan and Ron Schiffman. Seafood, simply and perfectly prepared, is this cafe's raison d'être, manifest in appetizers such as Dungeness crab legs Dijon, scallop ceviche redolent of lime and cilantro, or the choicest steamed clams and mussels in town. Entrees can be as unorthodox as scallops and shrimp sautéed with filberts, or as traditional as a lusty bouillabaisse. Salmon delicately broiled with lemon and capers, oysters tarragon, and (in a gesture to carnivores) rosemary-kissed rack of lamb accompanied by blueberry chutney, or grilled antelope topped with an Oregon blue cheese sauce—it's all good, and at times outstanding. However, we've withheld a star because consistency has slipped a bit lately, with some dishes arriving improperly cooked. Arrive early before the best choices are 86ed, and be ready to pay a high price for relatively small portions. Desserts can be sensational, particularly the white-chocolate torte bursting with marionberries. *1287 S Hemlock (at Dawes), Cannon Beach, OR 97110; (503)436-1179; $$$; beer and wine; AE, MC, V; checks OK; dinner every day (call for winter hours).*

IRA'S ★★

Higher rents and stiffer competition didn't stop Ira Mittelman from opening a Cannon Beach outpost of his inviting Astoria establishment. In fact, the new Ira's did so well that Mittelman decided to close the Columbia River shop and put all his efforts here. Since lunchtime is beach time, Mittelman now focuses on dinners. Expect to find some of the surprises you may have tasted in Astoria such as salmon-and-pepper pastas and 10-green salads dressed with feta, walnut, and sun-dried tomato vinaigrette, or tuna grilled with a peach barbecue sauce. Look for Cannon Beach innovations, such as the Ellensburg lamb with blue cheese and apple relish. Ira's side dishes and desserts are always standouts (especially on a summer's eve when you can dine on the deck). Time, we suspect, is all he needs here to win a few more stars in our book. *3401 S Hemlock, Tolovana Park, OR 97145; (503)436-1588; $$; full bar; MC, V; checks OK; dinner Wed–Mon (dinner every day in summer).*

MIDTOWN CAFE ★★

The secret's out about their favorite hangout, and Cannon Beachers don't like it one bit (sorry, we were just doing our job, ma'am). Even though they've made their cafe a little bit larger, it is still often tough to find enough stool space, so be one of the first to get there. The breakfast lineup here is legendary, with poppyseed waffles, corn-cheddar pancakes, oat scones, and kosher salami and eggs. Midday at the Midtown means fabulous soups such as Thai peanut, and unorthodox concoctions like tuna burritos. Be sure to grab a bagel, some gingerbread cookies, or some Haystack apple muffins, if the locals haven't gotten them all before you. *1235 S Hemlock (8 blocks south of downtown, on the east side of Hemlock, the main drag), Cannon Beach, OR 97110; (503)436-1016; $; beer and wine; no credit cards; local checks only; brunch Sun, breakfast, lunch Wed–Sat (closed Jan).*

THE BISTRO ★

Located in an alley off Hemlock Street, the Bistro is hard to find. But once inside, you'll enjoy its intimate interior, with hanging plants, open-beamed ceiling, and white-washed walls. You'll also appreciate the emphasis on fresh and simply prepared seafood. Dinners begin with a colorful antipasto plate (unusual at the beach), then move on to one of the daily soups (perhaps Greek lemon, robust black bean, or mushroom) or a simple salad. Salmon, which may be grilled with leeks and garnished with an understated garlic sauce, or coated with herbs and baked with sun-dried tomatoes, is top-notch. Consider also the farfalle pasta with shiitakes, cheese, and herbs. Service is on the slow side of casual, and lately some of the specials seem less than inspired, but the adjoining bar is a relaxing venue to catch a brew and order some garlic bread (with pizza sauce, Parmesan, and parsley) or grilled crab cakes finished with a sake-lemon butter. Occasional acoustic music, too. *263 N Hemlock (opposite Spruce, downtown), Cannon Beach, OR 97110; (503)436-2661; $$; full bar; MC, V; local checks only; dinner every day (closed Tues–Wed in winter).*

HOMEGROWN CAFE ☆

Hip, nutritious, and delicious, the Homegrown Cafe is reminiscent of a '60s-style healthnik eatery, but with a spiffed-up atmosphere and chow with pizzazz. There's a green-chile stew, breakfast burritos, English muffins topped with hot spiced apples, and "tease loaf," a meatloaf lookalike concocted from brown rice, mushrooms, nuts, and herbs. Aside from being good for you, this food is truly tasty. Ask the knowledgeable owners about the local music scene. *3301 S Hemlock (across the street from Tolovana Wayside Park), Tolovana Park, OR 97110; (503)436-1803; $; no alcohol; no credit cards; checks OK; breakfast, lunch Fri–Tues, dinner Fri–Mon.*

LAZY SUSAN CAFE ☆

Everyone in town seems to gather at this airy, sunny, double-deck restaurant in a courtyard opposite the Coaster Theater. The interior is bright with natural wood, plants hanging from the balcony, and local art on the walls. The tunes are New Age and the service is mellow. Breakfast is the best time here, when you can order sumptuous omelets (with egg whites only, if you want), oatmeal, waffles smothered with fresh fruit and yogurt, and excellent coffee to prolong your stay. Lunch (and occasionally dinner) options include quiche and some choice salads, including curried chicken with abundant fruit and a tangy mango chutney. Always worth

J.P.'s (1116 S Hemlock; (503)436-0908), connected to the Cannon Beach Hotel, sports a hip attitude. The open kitchen features a very theatrical chef (who manhandles fry pans awash with sherry) and a nice selection of tantalizing preparations. Reportedly, the halibut's first rate.

catching is the Mediterranean stew, a cioppinolike mixture of bay scallops, shrimp, and clams, blended with veggies and topped with melted cheese. Expect long waits on sunny weekends. *126 N Hemlock (downtown at Coaster Square), Cannon Beach, OR 97110; (503)436-2816; $; beer and wine; no credit cards; checks OK; breakfast, lunch every day, dinner Thurs–Sun.*

PIZZA A FETTA

It's easy to locate Cannon Beach's best pizza: Just follow the heady aroma of garlic, oregano, provolone, and pepperoni to this pint-size pizzeria, scrunched amid a maze of shops and galleries in the middle of downtown. The lineup ranges from a basic three-cheese pie to a white-clam concoction smothered with sun-dried tomatoes, mushrooms, cheeses, and lots of baby clams. Or create your own masterpiece with umpteen toppings including chorizo, pancetta, and a host of cheeses. For light eaters, the pizza is also offered by the slice. Or skip the pizza pie and dive into one of the 16 other kinds of pie. *231 N Hemlock Street, Cannon Beach, OR 97110; (503)436-0333; $; beer and wine; no credit cards, checks OK.*

LODGINGS

STEPHANIE INN

 This gorgeous oceanfront lodging radiates the elegance of a New England country inn. Situated amid other motels and residences, it's not isolated but feels exclusive. Inside, the emphasis is on pampered and purposeful service. Most of the 46 rooms include gas fireplaces, Jacuzzis (or smaller, one-person spas), VCRs, and stunning furnishings; the deck rooms on the third floor are the sunniest and most private. A full complimentary, buffet-style breakfast is served in the dining room. Come evening, Northwest wines are featured in the library. Watch the ocean, play the piano, or cozy up to the fireplace in the hotel's Chart Room. They've got all the pieces to a three-star puzzle and are on their way toward earning the extra star. Prix-fixe dinners are available to guests on a daily basis. There's a two-night minimum stay on Saturdays (and during the month of August). *2740 S Pacific (on the beach, at Matanuska and Pacific), Tolovana Park; (503)436-2221 or (800)633-3466; PO Box 219, Cannon Beach, OR 97110; stephinn@seasurf.com; www.seasurf.com~smmc; $$$; AE, DC, MC, V; checks OK.*

THE ARGONAUTA INN ☆

In downtown Cannon Beach, between bustling Hemlock Street and the beach, there are a confusing number of lodging options. The Argonauta, not really an inn but rather a cluster of five well-situated residences, is the best of the bunch. All units are nonsmoking and come equipped with comfy beds, pleasant furnishings, gas fireplaces, and color TVs. All but one have complete kitchens. The Lower Lighthouse, a cozy retreat for two, is the best deal, while the Chartroom sleeps four. The oceanfront Beach House, though expensive, is more like a miniature lodge (with a gas-fired river-rock fireplace, a spacious living room, two sun porches, three bedrooms, and two baths) and can accommodate 10 overnighters. Two suites within the Beach House, perfect for couples, are available at select times during the year. If the Argonauta is full, inquire about the Waves or the White Heron Lodge, nearby and under the same management. *188 W 2nd (corner of Larch), Cannon Beach; (503)436-2601 or (800)822-2468; PO Box 3, Cannon Beach, OR 97110; waves@seasurf.com; $$; DIS, MC, V; checks OK.*

CANNON BEACH HOTEL ☆

 Originally a boardinghouse, the Cannon Beach Hotel is a tidy, nine-room operation with a decidedly European flavor, including a cheery lobby (with lovely bunches of flowers, fresh fruit, hot beverages, and a fireplace) that's just right for lounging or light reading after a stroll on the nearby beach. The rooms are all designated as nonsmoking and vary from a nicely decorated, one-bed arrangement to a one-bedroom suite with a gas fireplace, spa, and ocean view. A newspaper and a light breakfast are brought to your door come morning. The more spendy

The Coaster Theater in Cannon Beach (108 N Hemlock; (503)436-1242) hosts year-round live entertainment, including touring musicians and theater productions.

Locals rely on the Upper Left Edge newspaper (free at many businesses) for town news and a cultural calendar, as well as a tide table.

Courtyard, a jointly managed lodging, offers more seclusion (with its out-of-the-wind brick courtyard) and is situated a tad closer to the ocean. J. P.'s (1116 S Hemlock, (503)436-0908), the restaurant adjacent to the Cannon Beach Hotel, is worth a visit regardless of where you're staying. It sports a hip attitude, with an open kitchen that features a theatrical chef (who manhandles fry pans awash with sherry), and serves up a nice selection of tantalizing preparations, including super salads and first-rate halibut and pastas. *1116 S Hemlock (corner of Gower), Cannon Beach; (503)436-1392; PO Box 943, Cannon Beach, OR 97110; $$; beer and wine; MC, V; checks OK; lunch, dinner every day (restaurant closed Sun in winter except holidays).*

SEA SPRITE GUEST LODGINGS ☆

This cute, always-popular oceanfront motel is a good getaway choice for couples or the family (but not for pets). Each of the five small but homey attached units includes a kitchen, color TV, and VCR. Most have woodstoves. A separate two-bedroom cottage with full kitchen sleeps eight. There's a picnic area and grill, as well as a washer and dryer on the premises. Firewood (well, a presto log), beach towels, and beach blankets are provided upon request. *280 Nebesna St (at Oceanfront), Tolovana Park; (503)436-2266; PO Box 933, Cannon Beach, OR 97110; $$; MC, V; checks OK.*

MCBEE MOTEL COTTAGES

Most lodgings in Cannon Beach are priced somewhere west of Pluto, but these charming attached cottages offer a reasonably priced respite from the nearby, sprawling "luxury" motels. Clean and comfy units can be had for less than $50. All 10 units enjoy curly-willow furniture and homey comforters and rugs; some have kitchens and fireplaces. Pets are welcome (for a $5 surcharge). The beach is but a block away and downtown a short stroll. In the winter, inquire about midweek, three-night specials. *888 S Hemlock (PO Box 943), Cannon Beach, OR 97110; (503)436-2569 or (800)238-4107; $; AE, DC, MC, V; checks OK.*

SURFSAND RESORT

An attractive beachfront complex, the Surfsand sits a short distance from Haystack Rock and the town's most crowded stretch of sand. Choose among an array of lodgings, including sleeping rooms, hyper-spendy suites (that sleep six), and separate houses (that can accommodate up to eight persons) located on the premises or sited around town. Most units have fireplaces; some sport kitchens and spas. All guests can soak in the indoor pool and spa and also receive complimentary use of the Cannon Beach Athletic Club facilities (located a couple of blocks away). The adjacent Wayfarer Restaurant has lots of oceanfront windows, a cozy lounge, and so-so chow; however, we like the summertime cabana service: They wait on you while you're at the beach. Pets are okay in some of the units. *Oceanfront at Grover (turn west at Hemlock and Grover), Cannon Beach; (503)436-2274 or (800)547-6100; PO Box 219, Cannon Beach, OR 97110; surfsand@seasurf.com; www.seasurf.com/~smmc; $$$; AE, MC, V; checks OK.*

"At the end of the summer, the tourists are in such a hurry to have a good time, they forget that they're here to relax."
—Mimi Kauffman, owner, Midtown Cafe

ARCH CAPE

Arch Cape marks the northern end of Cape Falcon, a well-known navigational landmark that juts 1.5 miles into the Pacific Ocean. The town is really no more than a post office with a deli; however, with miles of pristine beaches at your doorstep, some would argue, "Who needs more?"

ACTIVITIES

Beach Hikes. The Oregon Coast Trail winds up and over Arch Cape. The 8-mile segment of trail south of Arch Cape is the longest unbroken forested stretch of the Oregon Coast Trail. It veers to the inland side of Hwy 101 before crossing the highway as it makes the climb to Cape Falcon. The Cape Falcon Trail (an easy 2 miles one way) begins at Oswald West State Park, climbs through an old-growth forest of Sitka spruce, and ends at the tip of Cape Falcon. From here you can see Neahkahnie Mountain.

Historic Trail. Hug Point, located above Arch Cape and just 5 miles south of Cannon Beach, offers a fascinating look at how early settlers used the coast as a travel corridor. The Point had been used as a wagon road at low tide, but only after some judicious blasting cleared enough space to cross the headland. High tide will cause hikers to scramble up the beach to the highway in order to pass Hug Point.

LODGINGS

ST. BERNARDS ☆

Is it an English castle or a French chateau? You decide, but proprietors Don and Deanna Bernard roamed Europe for the furnishings gracing their palatial-looking lodging on the east side of Hwy 101. You might discover French provincial tables and lounge chairs (the Bernards spent their summers in Provence before moving here) or a 130-year-old Austrian bed (in the Ginger Room). All seven rooms have private baths, gas fireplaces, VCRs, and refrigerators. The top-floor Tower includes a spa and has the best view. Admire the handsome woodwork and wrought-iron lighting and door fixtures throughout the structure, or explore its numerous nooks and crannies and winding, castlelike stairways. Outside, there are trees on most sides, a sizable deck, and a windless courtyard. *3 E Ocean Rd (turn east off Hwy 101, across from the post office/grocery), Arch Cape; (503)436-2800 or (800)436-2848; PO Box 102, Arch Cape, OR 97102; $$$; AE, MC, V; checks OK.*

Janice Hondorp,
graphic artist and
designer, says her
favorite hike is
the Neahkahnie
Mountain trail: "It
takes me into a dif-
ferent world." Her
favorite mountain
biking in the Coast
Range includes the
grueling ride to
the top of Angora
Peak, which is
about 5 miles north-
east of Manzanita.

MANZANITA, NEHALEM, AND WHEELER

The Nehalem Bay area claims three small but appealing towns: Manzanita, Nehalem, and Wheeler. Resting mostly on a sandy peninsula with undulating dunes covered in beach grass, shore pine, and Scotch broom, Manzanita is a lazy but growing community gaining popularity as a coastal getaway for in-the-know urbanites. This tiny town on the northwestern side of Nehalem Bay is home to a surprisingly significant number of wealthy entrepreneurs and professionals, windsurfers, and excellent restaurants.

Nehalem is situated on the Nehalem River, which feeds into the bay. False-fronted buildings and friendly folks make up this town. Look for kayakers and fishermen enjoying the slow mouth of the river.

Wheeler flanks Nehalem Bay's southern end. If the rustic Australian-looking town seems vaguely familiar, it's because the town was featured in the movie *Point Break*.

ACTIVITIES

Visual Art. Check out the Osborne Gallery (635 Manzanita, Manzanita; (503)368-7518; very limited hours), featuring many of the owner's paintings. Nehalem's Three Village Gallery (35995 Hwy 101; (503)368-6924) exhibits sculpture, masks, pins, and a collection of decoys.

Quick Bites. Locals check in regularly at Manzanita News and Espresso (500 Laneda; (503)368-7450) for the relaxed ambience, the baked goodies, and, of course, a jolt of espresso. Another stop, offering more substantial fare, is Hill House Deli and Cafe (12870 Hwy 101, Nehalem; (503)386-7933).

Bar Scene. You'll find kicked-back, small-town atmosphere at Manzanita Sand-Dune Tavern (127 Laneda; (503)368-5080), offering pool tables, a gigantic river-rock fireplace, and a motley assortment of disenchanted yuppies and other local characters.

Stunning Hikes. Oswald West State Park (3 miles north of Manzanita on both sides of Hwy 101; (503)238-7488) is unsurpassed for scenic beauty in the Northwest, and laced with trails (suitable for hikers or adventuresome trail runners). A world-class hike begins half a mile south of the Arch Cape tunnel on the west side of the highway. It proceeds 5 miles over Cape Falcon to Short Sands Beach, a picture-perfect cove with a waterfall and steep, forested hillsides extending down to water level. Eventually, the trail crosses the highway and heads up to the 1,600-foot summit of Neahkahnie Mountain, the north coast's finest oceanfront panorama. The view from the top of Neahkahnie Mountain (2 switchbacked miles from trailhead to summit) is truly remarkable. For hikers who want to skip Cape Falcon and head for the views, the Neahkahnie Mountain trailhead is just off the east side of Hwy 101, 1.2 miles north of the exit to Neahkahnie Beach. Oswald West's camping area (the most secluded on the north coast; no reservations accepted) is situated half a mile down a paved trail from the parking area adjacent to Hwy 101, where wheelbarrows are available to transport your gear.

Favorite windsurfing spot: "Manzanita Beach—it rips when the wind's up."
—Dr. Larry Zagata, native Nehalemite

Board Heads. Manzanita's oceanfront and Nehalem Bay have become windsurfing meccas. Learn more at Manzanita Surf and Sail (150 Laneda; (503)368-7873), or ask the crew at Cassandra's pizza parlor, the favorite post-"rec" meltdown spot. Board surfers consider the cove at Short Sands Beach (within Oswald West State Park) a favorite spot, particularly in the summer. Long, gnarly rights break at the base of Neahkahnie Mountain, but it's rocky and conditions have to be just right to render it surfable. Surfboards and bodyboards are also available in Wheeler at Nehalem Bay Kayak Company; (503)368-6055.

Bike Loop. Nehalem Bay State Park (on the south end of Manzanita) offers miles of paved bike paths. Road bikers looking for a long-distance loop head south on Hwy 101 to Garibaldi, take the Miami River loop road to Mohler, then return to Hwy 101 and Nehalem and Manzanita (approximately 40 rolling miles). Rent bikes at Manzanita Fun Merchants (186 Laneda; (503)368-6606; with additional locations in Seaside and Cannon Beach). If it's flotsam and jetsam you're after, head to the southernmost day-use area of Nehalem Bay State Park (there's a parking fee charged in the summer). Take the short hike over the dune to the beach and head south, to the Nehalem River mouth and jetty.

Fishing. Fishermen flock to the Nehalem River for salmon and steelhead (particularly the North Fork, which is accessed off Hwy 53). The clamming and crabbing are good at Nehalem Bay. Stop in at the Nehalem Bay Chamber of Commerce in Wheeler for specifics on seasons and licenses; (503)368-5100.

Wildlife. Just south of Manzanita, extending for 4 miles from the north end of Nehalem Bay State Park to the Nehalem River jetty, is one of the better beachcombing stretches in Oregon. The river mouth is home to a vocal—and growing—seal and sea lion population. A designated whale-watching site in this area is at the historic marker turnout on Hwy 101 on Neahkahnie Mountain, north of Manzanita in Oswald West State Park.

Paddlers. Kayakers in Nehalem Bay won't claim it's anything like the San Juan Islands in Washington, but they still have lots of fun watching the waterfowl and maybe catching a glimpse of a resident seal or sea lion. Rent kayaks through Nehalem Bay Kayak Company in Wheeler (395 Hwy 101; (503)368-6055).

RESTAURANTS

BLUE SKY CAFE ★★★

The Blue Sky purveys a blend of cutting-edge Northwest, Southwest, Mediterranean, and Asian cuisines. Think Thai peanut chicken, smoked-duck quesadillas, and black-bean hummus. Also consider baked salmon in a mustard-seed vinaigrette, spinach spaghetti with sautéed pancetta and wild mushrooms, or succulent Gulf shrimp rolled in rice paper with pickled cucumber and spicy soy-roasted peanuts. For dessert, test the sugar-charged "thermonuclear chocolate device," a chocolate truffle cake with brownie crust, caramel sauce, and whipped cream. Even the decor is eclectic: Salt 'n' pepper shakers, ranging from miniature bowling pins to cow-driven tractors, grace every table while tiny, lime-green-lighted skeletons line the wine rack and dried peppers hang from the bar. The extensive wine list has an all-Oregon reserve pinot noir section but, alas, lists no vintages. This place is as far away from pretentious as you can get, but has incredibly inventive food. *154 Laneda Ave (at 2nd), Manzanita, OR 97130; (503)368-5712; $$$; full bar; no credit cards; checks OK; dinner Wed–Sun.*

"The Santa Fe chicken at Manzanita's Blue Sky is super, and their desserts are fabulous."
—Dr. Larry Zagata, native Nehalemite

JARBOE'S ☆☆☆

Outside, Jarboe's resembles a cute but humble beach bungalow. Inside, the decor is unassuming, with unobtrusive lighting and eight tables dressed with crisp white linens and small vases of flowers. Nothing whatsoever is allowed to upstage chef Klaus Monberg's French-inspired cuisine. Along with his wife, Suzanne Lange, the Danish-born, classically trained Monberg purveys a limited à la carte menu that changes—in some cases daily—depending on what foodstuffs are available. Look for intricate colors, textures, and flavors, and expect lots of mesquite-grilled meats and seafood. Appetizers range from a mussel terrine highlighted by basil and saffron to a crisp grilled flatbread with herbs and a mellow pecorino Romano. Crayfish complement a grilled salmon fillet enhanced with fennel, spinach, and dill, while sea scallops arrive skewered with mussels on a bed of red chard and slow-baked tomato confit. Desserts, such as Grand Marnier custard laced with raspberry sauce or a warm apple charlotte with crème Anglaise, are tantalizing. The exceptional wine list includes some stellar Oregon pinot noir choices. *137 Laneda Ave (at Carmel), Manzanita, OR 97130; (503)368-5113; $$$; beer and wine; MC, V; local checks only; dinner Thurs–Mon (Thurs–Sun in winter).*

CASSANDRA'S ☆☆

Under the direction of transplanted New Yorker Fawn de Turk, Cassandra's has evolved from a cool place to catch some hot pizza to an overall exceptional eatery (and the finest pizzeria on the Oregon Coast). Fawn chooses organic produce for her salads and toppings, and uses only meats and flour without preservatives for her hand-spun pizzas.

A couple of miles south of Manzanita, Nina's (Highway 101, Wheeler; (503) 368-6592) serves up hearty marinara-based lunches and dinners.

The colorful digs, just a block off the Manzanita ocean front, are a shrine to ocean play, decorated with vintage surfboards, saltwater paraphernalia, and imprints of water creatures. Pizzas range from traditional to way-different; the primavera pizza is outstanding. *60 Laneda Ave (1 block off the beach), Manzanita, OR 97130; (503)368-5593; $; beer and wine; no credit cards; checks OK; dinner every day.*

HERON ROCK

Just a couple of miles north of the famed Jarboe's, you'll find this bright little gem on the Newhalem River. It's fairly standard fare from halibut and chips to steaks, but best just to come, order one of their half-pound cheeseburgers, sit on the riverside deck, and listen to oldies. *380 Marine Dr, Wheeler, OR 97147; (503)368-7887; $$; full bar; DIS, MC, V; checks OK; breakfast Sat–Sun, lunch, dinner every day.*

LODGINGS

THE INN AT MANZANITA ☆☆

 One block off the beach, occupying a multilevel, woodsy setting similar to a Japanese garden, the Inn at Manzanita is a quiet, tranquil retreat. Each of the 13 spacious, nonsmoking units is finished in pine or cedar, with panels of stained glass here and there. Every room has a gas fireplace, a good-sized spa, a TV with VCR, a down comforter on the queen-size bed, and (except for the Hummingbird unit) a treetop ocean view. The Windrider features a vaulted ceiling and a paneled captain's bed (kind of like sleeping in an elegant sea chest). The newer and more modern-looking Cottage and Laneda units come with full kitchens and separate bedrooms. Extra touches include fresh flowers daily, terrycloth robes, and the morning paper at your doorstep. Two-night reservations are required in summer. *67 Laneda Ave (1 block from the beach), Manzanita, OR 97130; (503)368-6754; $$$; MC, V; checks OK.*

OCEAN INN ☆☆

 You'd have to sleep on the beach to get any closer than this to Manzanita's ocean waves. Remodeled (with six additional rooms) and ultra-attractive, the Ocean Inn offers 10 one-bedroom units, all nonsmoking. The cottagelike older units (No. 1 is nicest, with a beachfront living room and sheltered deck) are nearer the ocean and feature knotty pine interiors, good-sized kitchens (with microwaves), woodstoves or fireplaces, and foldout futons. The spacious—and gorgeous—newer lodgings (No. 9 is our favorite) boast vaulted ceilings with stained-glass chandeliers, sound-resistant walls, vertical-grain fir woodwork, and beautiful craftsmanship throughout. Some have full kitchens and wood heaters. No. 10 is fully equipped for persons with disabilities. Covered parking is provided for all guests. One-week minimum stay is usually required in July and August. *20 Laneda Ave (on the beach), Manzanita, OR 97130; (503)368-6797 or (800)579-9801; PO Box 162, Manzanita, OR 97130; $$$; MC, V; checks OK.*

GARIBALDI AND BAY CITY

This is Tillamook County, home to four bays: Nehalem, Tillamook, Netarts, and Nestucca. Tillamook Bay—which fronts Garibaldi and Bay City—is the largest and most accessible, and one of the seasonal homes for the summer salmon fleet—or what's left of it, pending ever-increasing government restrictions on commercial fishing. The towns are reaching out for more tourist business to supplement their traditional, but diminishing, logging and fishing income.

ACTIVITIES

Trophy Fish. The Ghost's Hole section of Tillamook Bay, halfway between Garibaldi and Bay City, routinely yields 30-plus-pound chinook salmon. The Kilchis River, just south of Bay City, is another trophy salmon stream. Barview County Park (off Hwy 101 at Barview, just north of Garibaldi) affords excellent jetty fishing. The Miami River (at Garibaldi's south end) is a noted trout stream. Pier's End fishing pier in Garibaldi offers wheelchair access out over deep water for bottom fishing. Scuba divers also make use of the pier, one of the few dive sites in Oregon that doesn't require a boat. Tidal currents can be strong near the mouth of the bay, and divers should be experienced. Garibaldi is also the headquarters of the bay's large fleet of charter boats. Although salmon continue to be sought offshore, many of the trips seek bottom fish and halibut. One of Oregon's most productive halibut areas lies 20 miles off the entry to Tillamook Bay. Clams and crabs are numerous in Tillamook Bay, as well as in Nehalem, Netarts, and Nestucca Bays. Species of bay clams include cockle, littleneck, butter, and softshell. Razor clams are usually found on sandy stretches of coastal beaches. Oregon's food crabs are Dungeness and red rock. Clamming and crabbing do not require licenses, but both activities have a long list of regulations that must be observed. Garibaldi Marina (302 Mooring Basin Rd, Garibaldi; (503)322-3312) rents boats and equipment, sells bait, and provides information.

Fresh Seafood. Harvesting native oysters is not allowed in Oregon, and cultured oysters are private property that require the owner's permission to collect. For fresh local oysters and seafood to take home with you, head to Miller Seafood (along Hwy 101; (503)322-0355) or Smith's Pacific Shrimp Company (608 Commercial; (503)322-3316), both in Garibaldi. Or have them served up fresh at the Artspace Gallery Cafe (see review below), located in a converted meat market. For a taste on the go, pick some 'sters up at Pacific Oyster Company (5150 Oyster Drive, Bay City; (503)377-2323) and have a picnic on the adjacent pier.

Whale Watching. Because resident whales frequently frolic in the kelp beds near shore, it's always wise to watch for them whenever you visit the Oregon Coast. Several coastal charter boat services, however, have expanded their business to include whale-watching trips. Check with D&D Charters in Garibaldi, (503)322-0381, about catching sight of the big grays from Tillamook Bay.

RESTAURANTS

ARTSPACE GALLERY CAFE ☆

Here's a novel idea: Combine an avant-garde art gallery exhibiting wooden carvings, marble sculptures, and wild-colored multimedia paintings with an appealing eatery. The art gallery may change exhibits every month or so but the food is always irresistible. Gallery steps lead down to an intimate, bistrolike setting where a young and attentive waitstaff brings meals on octagonal glass tableware. Succulent Tillamook Bay oysters, lightly breaded, garlicked, and grilled or baked Italian-style with herbs and cheeses, are the limited menu's star attractions. But you'll also find a trio of fettuccines, baked chicken lightly bathed in lemon, and a couple of fresh-fish choices (and a tempting shrimp cocktail). Soups (such as the nectar-sweet carrot porridge) and even simple salads are as enlightening as the artwork. An outside deck provides an opportunity for sunny-day sipping and supping. *9120 5th St (Hwy 101 and 5th), Bay City, OR 97107; (503)377-2782; $; beer and wine; no credit cards; checks OK; lunch every day, dinner Thurs–Sat, brunch Sun.*

DOWNIE'S CAFE

Take a step back to the '50s in this neighborhood cafe offering down-home service and food. The place is patronized mostly by locals, who clamor for Downie's clam chowder, a thick, creamy potion of potatoes, celery, and clam chunks. Fish 'n' chips are greasy good fun, the burgers are humongous (try the oyster burger), and the pies are yum-worthy. *9320 5th St, Bay City, OR 97107; (503)377-2220; $; no alcohol; no credit cards; checks OK; breakfast, lunch every day.*

TILLAMOOK AND OCEANSIDE

A broad, flat expanse of bottomland created by the confluence of three rivers (the Tillamook, Trask, and Wilson), Tillamook is best known as dairy country. Downtown still looks like a working farm town rather than a tourist town. Eight miles west and quaint as can be, tiny Oceanside is Tillamook's beach resort.

Cape Lookout, in Cape Meares State Park, is a large jewel in Oregon's park system, with 250 campsites, headland-hugging trails, and a huge stretch of little-used beach.

ACTIVITIES

Cheese Tours. Things can get cheesy around here, especially at the north end of town, where you'll find the Tillamook County Creamery Association plant and visitors center (4175 Hwy 101 N; (503)842-4481). The tour is self-guided, but there's not a whole lot to see. Still, the place is almost always crowded. The Blue Heron Cheese Company (2001 Blue Heron Dr; (503)842-8281), about a mile south, is stocked with a variety of cheeses and other made-in-Oregon munchies. There's also a wine-tasting room for Northwest wines.

Forest Grove to Tillamook Scenic Drive. The Wilson River Hwy, which runs between Tillamook and Forest Grove on Hwys 6 and 8, is one of the most beautiful ways to cross the Coast Range in Oregon. The highway passes many tempting riverside settings as well as hiking trails up one of the finest mountains in the Coast Range. The Elk Mountain Trail (a difficult 4 miles round trip) begins at Elk Mountain Campground on the north side of Hwy 6, 5 miles west of the Coast Range summit. The King's Mountain Trail (a difficult 5 miles round trip) is on the north side of the highway, 2 miles north of Elk Mountain Campground.

Tidepooling. Although whales are the star attraction, tide pools also offer an interesting and fun wildlife encounter. Tide pools around Tillamook can be found on the south sides of each of the three capes—Meares, Lookout, and Kiwanda. The Kiwanda tide pools are relatively easy to reach from the beach, but the Meares tide pools require a hike north of Short Beach, which is 1 mile north of Oceanside, and the Lookout tide pools are 2.5 miles south from the trailhead where the Three Capes

Even though they have to contend with minimal shoulder space and lung-searing climbs, bicyclists favor the Three Capes loop. Check individual park regulations to see if off-road riding is permitted on cape trails.

Scenic Drive crosses the headland. Maxwell Point at Oceanside offers easy access to tide pools.

Three Capes Scenic Drive. The 22-mile Three Capes Scenic Drive, which begins west of Tillamook, is one of Oregon's most beautiful stretches of coastline. The narrow, winding road skirts the outline of Tillamook Bay, climbs over Cape Meares, and brushes past Oceanside. The route then traverses the shores of Netarts Bay before scaling the steep slope of Cape Lookout. Spectacular ocean vistas fill the drive down the south side of the cape. Back at sea level lies a desertlike landscape of sandy dunes. The road to Pacific City and the route's third cape, Kiwanda, runs through lush, green dairy country.

Dunes. Sandlake, between Cape Lookout and Pacific City along Three Capes Scenic Drive, is mainly a gas station and a grange hall. But it's also the gateway to thousands of acres of sandy dunes, where off-road vehicle enthusiasts come to play. You're allowed to drive only in designated areas, and regulations are posted. The Forest Service operates 101 campsites (closed during the winter) at the Sandbeach Campground.

Migrating Whales. One of the best places to view whales is the tip of Cape Lookout, accessible by a 2.5-mile trail from the mainland and one of 29 state designated whale-watching sites along the Oregon Coast. The trail has several good views down into the ocean on the south side of the cape, as well as expansive views to the south and west. Trained volunteers, working in cooperation with the Oregon Department of Fish and Wildlife and the Oregon Parks and Recreation Department, are on hand twice each year at these sites to help visitors spot migrating California gray whales. Although the whale migration lasts several weeks and a few whales are year-round residents, Oregon's official whale-watching weeks are timed to coincide with school holidays: the week between Christmas and New Year's for the southward migration, and March spring break for the northward trip. Migrating whales can be seen for two or three weeks on either side of these holidays. (These weeks also coincide with the coastal winter and spring storm seasons, so not every day is a good day to look for whales.) The whale-watching program is run by the Department of Fish and Wildlife's Newport office; (541) 867-4741. Whales are typically a mile or more offshore, so it takes a powerful pair of binoculars to locate them. Observers watch for plumes of spray the whales exhale from their blowholes when they surface to breathe. Whales can occasionally be seen much closer to shore, especially where they round headlands that jut far out into the ocean, like Cape Lookout. Another good spot in this area: Detour from the Three Capes Scenic Drive into Oceanside to the top of Maxwell Mountain (a road leads up) for a stunning vantage point of the Pacific and of migrating gray whales (also a favored launching spot for hang gliders).

Scenic Trails. Cape Meares State Park offers a cliff-skirting section of the Oregon Coast Trail, and a paved jaunt down to the Cape Meares Lighthouse (which is open to the public), from which the view, especially at sunset, is breathtaking. Seals and sea lions frolic on the rock reefs below. Be sure to visit the Octopus Tree, a giant Sitka spruce formerly used as a Native American burial tree. Drive to the crest of Cape Lookout (or hike from sea level) and pick up the 3-mile-long trail to the cape's tip for an awesome ocean vista from the western-most headland on the north Oregon Coast. Along the way the trail meanders through primeval forests of stately cedar, western hemlock, and Sitka spruce. Farther south, Cape Kiwanda is a mass of wave-sculpted sandstone cliffs, sand dunes, and sea-level tide pools.

Delightful Detour. Beaver, a logging hamlet 15 miles south of Tillamook along Hwy 101, is the jump-off point for the Upper Nestucca River Recreation Area and several Forest Service campgrounds. Adventuresome travelers can drive (or bike) the 51 miles all the way to Willamina, on the western edge of the Willamette Valley. The mostly paved road follows the Nestucca River upstream through old-growth remnant forests and sees very little traffic.

Off-road Adventures. The 364,000-acre Tillamook State Forest is best known for its off-road vehicle riding opportunities for four-wheel drives, four-wheelers, and motorcycles. Despite the noise the vehicles make, Tillamook State Forest is a very large place capable of comfortably handling hikers,

Canoeists and kayakers can wet their paddles on either side of the Bayocean Peninsula, which divides Tillamook Bay from the ocean.

*The Tillamook
Naval Air Station
Museum (off
Highway 101 south
of town; (503)842-
1130) has an excel-
lent World War II
plane collection,
which is housed in
one of the world's
largest wooden,
clear-span build-
ings, a former
blimp hangar.*

equestrians, mountain bikers, and fishermen along with the ORV crowd. There's also good family camping. In the Tillamook State Forest there is the 9-mile Wilson River Wagon Route Trail, which begins across Hwy 6 from the entrance to Elk Creek Campground and follows the south side of Hwy 6. It is open to bicycles, horses, and hikers, but is one of the few trails along the highway's south side that is off-limits to motorized vehicles. Generally speaking, the Tillamook State Forest is open to ORVs south of Hwy 6 and closed on the north side of the highway. Hwy 6 is a convenient dividing line for the two different types of recreation.

Fishing. Tillamook Bay and the surrounding countryside provide outstanding angling opportunities. The Wilson, Tillamook, and Trask Rivers are superb salmon and steelhead streams. A popular, easily accessible fishing section of the Tillamook River is located adjacent to a state wayside area (with rest rooms), 3 miles south of Tillamook just off Hwy 101. Wilson River is consistently a top producer of salmon and steelhead. Never far from Hwy 6, the river has good access. There are spring runs, but the fall runs tend to be bigger and last longer. (Steelhead are in the river year-round, but winter is the most productive time.) Contact The Guide Shop (12140 Wilson River Hwy near Tillamook; (503)642-3474).

Family Walk. Munson Creek Waterfall (266 feet high) is the highest in Oregon's Coast Range. The half-mile trail to the waterfall begins at Munson Falls County Park, 1.6 miles east of Hwy 101 at the community of Pleasant Valley (7 miles south of Tillamook). It's a wonderful and easy side trip for adventurous families young and old.

RESTAURANTS

ROSEANNA'S OCEANSIDE CAFE   ☆

 Thank goodness there's a worthwhile restaurant in pretty, pint-size (and noncommercialized) Oceanside. Outside, Roseanna's is a converted country grocery fronted by wooden walkways and a funky facade. But inside, pastel tones, polished service, and an upscale menu lend an urbane air. Order tiger prawns or Tillamook Bay oysters with one of three sauces, including a zippy sesame oil, ginger, and jalapeño concoction. Halibut or salmon (cod and snapper, too) might be finished with an apricot-ginger or a Dijon-citrus glaze, while the "big salad" is a cornucopia of vegetables and greens blended with crab, cod, shrimp, or chicken. Steaks, pasta, quiche (try the veggie, herb, and Swiss), and some top-drawer clam chowder are menu stalwarts. Look for warm Toll House pie topped with Tillamook ice cream for dessert. Dining-room views of the ocean and nearby Three Arch Rocks make meals more memorable. *1490 Pacific St (on Ocean-side's main drag), Oceanside, OR 97134; (503)842-7351; $$; full bar; MC, V; checks OK; lunch, dinner every day.*

LODGINGS

HOUSE ON THE HILL

 Bring your binoculars. The setting, on a 250-foot-high bluff overlooking Three Arch Rocks (a bird, seal, and sea lion sanctuary) and the blue Pacific, is unbeatable. The "house" is actually a collection of buildings, with 16 units (all with refrigerators and ocean vistas) and a honeymoon suite. Nothing fancy, but the views are tops. Choose a unit with a kitchen and stock up on groceries in Tillamook. The Rock Room, with telescopes to spy on the wildlife and scan the horizon for whales, is open to all guests. Kids are fine for some units (but call ahead). *1816 Maxwell Mountain Rd (at Maxwell Point), Oceanside; (503)842-6030; PO Box 187, Oceanside, OR 97134; $$; MC, V; no checks.*

CLOVERDALE AND PACIFIC CITY

Three Capes Scenic Drive rejoins Hwy 101 just outside Pacific City, home of the dory fleet (Oregon's oceangoing salmon-fishing boats, which are launched from the beach at Cape Kiwanda). Cloverdale, a dairy community tucked into the lush Nestucca River valley, is a couple of miles north on Hwy 101.

ACTIVITIES

Ocean Fishing. The ultimate fishing trip in Tillamook County, even in all of Oregon, is to launch from the beach in a Pacific City dory. The Haystack Fishing Club, (503)965-7555, offers trips through the surf in the dories. Fishing is for salmon, halibut, lingcod, and bottom fish. It's a five-hour fishing adventure, customized to your needs. The highly mobile dory fleet also schedules whale-watching tours that begin on the beach at Pacific City, plus dory rides on local rivers and river fishing trips. Although dories can be launched elsewhere along the coast, Pacific City is the only U.S. town on the Pacific Ocean that is home to a commercial fleet of these appealing boats.

River Angling. More salmon and steelhead are taken from the Nestucca River than any other comparably sized stream in Oregon. The river's accessible from Hwy 101 between Beaver and Pacific City. The Little Nestucca River, south of Pacific City and accessible from a secondary road that parallels the river, is another excellent angling prospect.

Hiking. Cape Kiwanda, at the north end of Pacific City, offers myriad hiking opportunities, all of them sandy (4 miles of beach reach south along the Nestucca Spit). Park at the adjacent Cape Kiwanda State Park (day-use only) and head on up the sandy slopes. Watch for hang gliders swooping off the cape from above.

Views. There's always a crowd of view-seekers at Cape Kiwanda, but if it's solitude you're after, head north a couple of miles on Three Capes Scenic Drive to the cliffside turnout just north of the tiny beach community of Tierra del Mar. You just might have the spot—and the beach below—to yourself.

A Forest Find. Hebo Lake, nestled at the 1,700-foot-level of Mount Hebo, is a secluded forest paradise (that gets a lot of winter moisture). There's a campground, a fishing dock, and a reconstructed pioneer shelter. Hebo Lake is 5 miles from Hebo (along Hwy 101, 2 miles north of Cloverdale), on paved Forest Service Rd 14. Trails lead into primitive sections of the Coast Range.

Robert Straub State Park is situated at the south end of Pacific City and occupies most of the Nestucca beach sand spit, an excellent beachcombing locale.

RESTAURANTS

GRATEFUL BREAD BAKERY ☆

Transplanted New Yorkers Laura and Gary Seide tempt you with robust breads, muffins, and a scrumptious array of sweets—carrot cake and gargantuan cinnamon rolls, to name a couple—in a cheerful, beachy setting. There are extensive breakfast and lunch menus that list gingerbread pancakes, a hangtown fry bursting with oysters, and some very cheesy New York–style pizza. Other options include veggie lasagna, a few hearty soups, and an array of imaginative sandwiches (try the untraditional ham or turkey "Reuben"). Enjoy your coffee and cake out on the deck, and grab a loaf of bread or a baguette for the road. *34805 Brooten Rd (on the Pacific City loop road), Pacific City, OR 97315; (503)965-7337; $; no alcohol; MC, V; checks OK; breakfast, lunch every day (closed in Jan and Wed–Thurs in other winter months).*

Sea kayakers paddle into the Pacific in the lee of Cape Kiwanda (the same route the dories take) to begin a good wave workout.

PELICAN PUB AND BREWERY

The best spot for soaking up Cape Kiwanda's geographical splendor is this bright and airy beachfront pub. In-house craft brews include Kiwanda cream ale, Doryman's dark ale, Tsunami stout, and an unfiltered wheat brew called "Heiferweizen" (remember, this is cow country). Finger foods range from warm, garlicky bread sticks to deep-fried clam strips. Beefy chili, a tempting sandwich lineup (try the charbroiled chicken), and a selection of thin-crusted pizzas coated with gobs of mozzarella and Tillamook cheeses round out the fare. *33180 Cape Kiwanda Dr (on the beach at Cape Kiwanda), Pacific City,*

OR 97315; (503)965-7007; $; beer and wine; AE, DC, MC, V; checks OK; breakfast, lunch, dinner every day.

RIVERHOUSE RESTAURANT

You might see a great blue heron perched on a log on the Nestucca River, which flows idly to the sea right outside the window. The Riverhouse is a calming stop, 3 miles off Hwy 101, and far removed from the typical tourist trappings. It's small—10 or so tables—with hanging plants and a piano in the corner for local musicians, who perform on weekends. The sizable menu (especially for such a diminutive place) ranges from hot tuna or broiled asparagus (with Jack and Parmesan cheeses) sandwiches to crepes Florentine or a bucket of steamers. Don't miss the apple pie or the frosty ice-cream floats. *34450 Brooten Rd (¼ mile north of the stoplight on Brooten Rd), Pacific City, OR 97315; (503)965-6722; $$; full bar; MC, V; checks OK; lunch, dinner every day (closed in Dec).*

LODGINGS

HUDSON HOUSE BED AND BREAKFAST ☆☆

Perched on a bluff in the middle of nowhere, the picturesque Hudson House, built in 1906 and on the National Register of Historic Places, evokes memories of a country weekend at Grandma's. The entire restored Victorian farmhouse is dedicated to the guests. The four guest rooms are decorated in an early-20th-century country style (brass beds, claw-footed tubs, and gabled ceilings) and look out on forested hillsides surrounding the pastoral Nestucca River valley, prime dairy country. Breakfasts are exceptional, including unusual treats such as cheese casseroles, apple-filled puff pancakes, and homemade Wholly Cow cereal. Pacific City, Cape Kiwanda, and the ocean are 3 miles away. *37700 Hwy 101 S (2½ miles south of Cloverdale), Cloverdale, OR 97112; (503)392-3533; $$; AE, MC, V; checks OK.*

EAGLE'S VIEW BED AND BREAKFAST

 Eagles may perch here; it's certainly high enough, overlooking Nestucca Bay and the surrounding dairy and forest lands. More than likely, though, one of Mike and Kathy Lewis's dachshunds or Siamese cats will offer a polite greeting after you ascend the steep driveway and multi-leveled staircase to this secluded B&B. Five guest rooms, furnished with comfy chairs and cheery, handcrafted (by Kathy) quilts, are available. All have private baths, three enjoy spas, and one is wheelchair accessible. Full breakfasts can be had in the privacy of your room, or join others in the sizable downstairs dining area or out on the porch and decks, where the panoramas are grand. *37975 Brooten Rd (½ mile west of Hwy 101), Pacific City; (503)965-7600 or (888)846-3292; PO Box 901, Pacific City, OR 97135; www.moriah.com/inns; $$; DIS, MC, V; checks OK.*

INN AT CAPE KIWANDA

 This new 35-room hotel is a nice addition to Pacific City. Most of the rooms are on the second and third floors, so they all have ocean views and patios (retail space and a coffee shop fill the street level). The suite (the only one with its own kitchen) sleeps up to four, but our pick for the price are the Jacuzzi rooms with gas fireplaces. With only a two-lane road and a parking lot between you and the beach, it's about the closest beach bunk you'll get in this town. *33105 Cape Kiwanda Dr, Pacific City, OR 97315; (503)965-7001; $$$; MC, V; checks OK.*

The view from the top of Mount Hebo (elevation about 3,100 feet), a couple of miles up the road from Hebo Lake, is singular; Hebo Ranger District, 31525 Highway 22, PO Box 325, Hebo, OR 97122; (503)392-3161.

NESKOWIN

Neskowin is a diminutive, mostly residential community lying in the lee of Cascade Head—a steeply sloped and forested promontory. Neskowin affords the final refuge before the touristy "20 miracle miles" (as the stretch from Lincoln City to Newport was formerly called). The beach here is narrower, but decidedly less crowded, than other locales.

ACTIVITIES

Rain Forests and Meadows. Majestic Cascade Head has miles of lonely hiking trails that traverse rain forests and meadows, then skirt rocky cliffs with breathtaking vistas. They begin at a marked trailhead about 2 miles south of Neskowin (visible from Hwy 101). Forest Service Rd 1861, also called Cascade Head Rd (which intersects Hwy 101 at the top of Cascade Head), leads to the Harts Cove Trail, that drops 800 feet from the end of the road to a bluff overlooking the inaccessible shores of the cove.

Creative Travel. The nonprofit Sitka Center for Art and Ecology (turn on Three Rocks Rd off Hwy 101, then to Ridge Rd, Neskowin; (541)994-5485) operates on the south side of Cascade Head and offers art and writing classes (from watercolors and printmaking to poetry and woodcarving) plus numerous talks and exhibits. The classes are usually one to three days, perfect for creative visitors and locals.

Biking. The Neskowin Scenic Route, an enchanting alternative to Hwy 101, winds through horse farms and old-growth forests before rejoining the main road at Otis (a couple of miles east of Hwy 101). The route is narrow, with lots of climbing and switchbacks. Mountain bikers can climb to the top of Cascade Head on Cascade Head Rd (Forest Service Rd 1861).

RESTAURANTS

OTIS CAFE ☆

The sole reason to visit Otis, a blacktop blink just south of Neskowin and 2 miles east of Hwy 101, is to dine at the Otis Cafe, a hugely popular, retro eatery with no-frills food at old-fashioned prices. Contented diners (no one leaves here hungry) nosh on beefy burgers, thick 'n' chunky soups, filling breakfasts (including plate-sized portions of hashbrowns, onions, peppers, and melted cheese), and huge malts and milk shakes. Dinner offerings include fish, pork chops, and chicken-fried steak. The buttery black bread is sold to go, in case you can't get enough of it while you're there; other baked items, especially the pies, are delish. *Hwy 18, Otis Junction (¼ mile from Otis Junction), Otis, OR 97368; (541)994-2813; $; beer and wine; AE, MC, V; checks OK; breakfast, lunch, dinner every day (dinner Fri–Sun in winter).*

The Hawk Creek Cafe (4505 Salem, Neskowin; (503)392-3838) is your best bet for a beer or a glass of wine, as well as an outdoor deck with a great view.

LODGINGS

THE CHELAN   ☆

This attractive white-and-blue adobe structure encompasses nine condominium units, all with lovely ocean views. Private homes are nearby, but this place feels like a getaway retreat. There's a manicured front lawn, lush gardens, and a secluded atmosphere. Every one of the nine condos has a well-equipped kitchen, a large living room with a picture window, and a brick fireplace. Most have two bedrooms. Ground-floor units have a private entrance to a small backyard, with the ocean just beyond. Upstairs accommodations (off-limits to children) enjoy private balconies. No pets. *48750 Breakers Blvd (just off Salem Blvd), Neskowin, OR 97149; (503)392-3270; $$$; MC, V; checks OK.*

Vehicles are not allowed on the beach from north of Lincoln City near Neskowin all the way south to Florence.

PACIFIC SANDS

A stone's throw from breaking waves, this well-maintained condo-motel with an average, bland exterior enjoys a super setting, although development is encroaching on either side. Only 10 of the condos are for rent; each has a fireplace, kitchen, and more than enough room to stretch out and get comfortable. Opt for a beachfront unit (if available), and step out to miles of untrampled sand. *48250 Breakers Blvd (at Amity), Neskowin; (503)392-3101; PO Box 356, Neskowin, OR 97149; $$; MC, V; checks OK.*

LINCOLN CITY

There are two state parks, two waysides, and 10 city parks, all within the city limits. On the south end of town, pull into Siletz Bay Park for a sunset picnic.

There is no off-season here. Every weekend is crowded, and traffic can be the pits. Hwy 101 just wasn't designed for so many vehicles, and the congestion has local and Oregon Department of Transportation officials helplessly throwing their hands in the air. A slew of factory outlet stores (more than 50 at last count) located halfway through town has created additional gridlock. However, with more people comes more opportunity. In fact, today Lincoln City offers more tourist accommodations than any other Oregon Coast city (and a high percentage of ocean-view rooms).

ACTIVITIES

Kite Culture. Kite flying is a popular pastime in this beach town, and so are festivals celebrating the art of flying a kite. Lincoln City usually stages kite festivals in the spring and fall at the D River Wayside, one of the smallest but busiest Oregon state parks. Really little more than a highway rest area, the park offers access to Lincoln City's miles of coastal sand. There's a spring kite festival in May, a stunt kite version in July, and an international kite festival in October (Lincoln City Visitor and Convention Bureau, 801 SW Hwy 101; (800)452-2151). Also stop by Catch the Wind Kite Shop (266 SE Hwy 101; (541)994-9500), headquarters for a kite manufacturing company, which has eight outlets along the coast.

Local Arts and Crafts. The Ryan Gallery, on the north side of town (4270 NE Hwy 101; (541)994-5391), offers an eclectic artwork collection. Mossy Creek Pottery in Kernville, just south of Lincoln City (a half mile up Immonen Rd; (541)996-2415), sells some of the area's best locally made high-fired stoneware and porcelain.

Endless Beach. Beginning at Roads End, a state wayside allows parking and beach access at the north end of town (a far better choice for solitude than D River Wayside). There are 7 miles of continuous sandy beach for hiking, running, and beachcombing, all the way to Siletz Bay. Throughout the Lincoln City area, numerous streets (which intersect Hwy 101) offer beach access. Most offer limited parking.

Hang 10, Too. The Roads End area (on Lincoln City's north side) and the Nelscott area (on the south side, below the Inn at Spanish Head) offer surfing potential. Stop at the Oregon Surf Shop (4933 SW Hwy 101; (541)996-3957), which houses the largest board inventory in the state.

D River (a 400-foot-long stretch from Devil's Lake to the beach) is said to be the shortest river in the world.

Fishing. Lake, river, or ocean—whichever is your fishing preference, Lincoln City has it all. Devil's Lake (the site of a state park) is a fisherman's heaven, as it is stocked with trout and also offers bass, catfish, and perch. The Siletz River is a salmon, steelhead, and trout stream. Surf fishing is popular along the beaches of the Siletz River estuary.

Day Trips. Short, little-known side trips (both south of town) will recharge your spirits after enduring Lincoln City's commercial blitz. The Drift Creek covered bridge is reached via Drift Creek Rd (a half mile south of the city limits off Hwy 101). A little way south lies the Kernville junction and Hwy 229. Take this road less than a half mile for a view of the restored Victorian house used in the movie set for *Sometimes a Great Notion*.

Seal Watching. A pod of harbor seals frequently pulls up and basks in the sun at the southern entrance to Siletz Bay. One of the best places to view the seals is from Taft Waterfront Park, which sits at the north end of Siletz Bay only a short walk from the coastal beach. Bring binoculars.

Valley of the Giants. This 47-acre old-growth forest preserve is one hike that shouldn't be missed, but it's easy to miss because it's tough to find. Those who do have an incredible sight awaiting them, as this is home to some of Oregon's oldest trees. The valley has a dozen Douglas fir and western hemlock with 25-foot girths. The hiking loop is 1.7 miles. Contact the Bureau of Land Management's Mary's Peak Resource Area in Salem for directions; (541)375-5646.

RESTAURANTS

BAY HOUSE ☆☆☆

 Shoreside restaurants with spectacular views can often get away with serving overpriced, mediocre food. Happily,

Why not head to the source? The ambience isn't that enticing (right in the middle of a strip mall), but the Lighthouse Brewpub (4157 N Highway 101; (503)994-7238) handcrafts some alluring ales and offers as many as 25 beers on tap.

"One of my favorite things to do here is to walk along the shore of Siletz Bay."
—*Leslie Dressel, proprietor, Bay House Restaurant*

this is not the case at the Bay House, located on the banks of Siletz Bay, just out of reach of the glitzy Lincoln City tourist trade. The ambience is traditional—crisp tablecloths and lots of richly finished wood and brass. The seasonal menu features mostly seafood, sometimes in imaginative preparations such as a grilled catch of the day with shiitake and oyster mushrooms in a Bordeaux sauce, along with a blue cheese potato pancake. Salmon might be highlighted by a hazelnut crust, while halibut could be brushed with Parmesan, baked, and served on a lily white béchamel sauce. Oysters, scallops, Dungeness crab legs (served with angel hair pasta)—they're all afforded reverential treatment. So, too, is rack of lamb roasted in an herb crust with port demiglace. Alongside the grilled pork loin stuffed with andouille sausage (accompanied by apple-currant compote) and the portobello mushrooms bathed in a pomegranate vinaigrette are splendidly simple dishes such as penne pasta tossed with seasonal veggies and herb-infused olive oil. Desserts (lemon-almond cheesecake or tiramisu, for instance) are ethereal. Time your reservations with sunset, and experience the solace of Siletz Bay. *5911 SW Hwy 101 (at the south edge of town), Lincoln City, OR 97367; (541)996-3222; $$$; full bar; AE, MC, V; checks OK; dinner every day (Wed–Sun in winter).*

CHAMELEON CAFE ☆

This small storefront cafe packs one heck of a culinary punch, with plenty of variety. Reggae or Caribbean tunes emanate from the sound system, and the interior is sparsely decorated with outrageous art and patrolled by hip waitresses. The intriguing menu features dishes such as wild rice-mushroom cakes with aioli, and red onions and hot artichoke paté. Brie quesadillas and spicy fish tacos accompanied by black beans, rice, and a scintillating salsa highlight the south-of-the-border selections. Mediterranean cuisine is also in evidence, including various pasta dishes (try the penne with smoked salmon and pine nuts), a super-garlicky hummus served with pita crisps, and marinated eggplant sandwiches. *2145 NW*

Hwy 101 (on the west side of Hwy 101), Lincoln City, OR 97367; (541)994-8422; $; beer and wine; DIS, MC, V; checks OK; lunch, dinner Mon–Sat.

SALMON RIVER CAFE ☆

Part deli, part bistro, this is the place for picnic fixings and quality fast food. A large glass case displays unusual salads, pastas, and desserts, including bread pudding and chocolate pots de crème. Pastries, such as buttermilk scones and some mighty fine cinnamon rolls, adorn the counter. Sit-down diners will prize the cheerful service and the tempting aromas wafting from the open kitchen, presided over by Barbara Lowry (who formerly headed the kitchen at the Bay House). Breakfast features smoked salmon and scrambled eggs served with rosemary-and-garlic-kissed potatoes; lunch offerings include Italian-inspired sandwiches and Lincoln City's finest cheeseburgers; dinner (oysters with risotto, for example) will make you want to return the next morning. Browse the Italian and Northwest wine selection while waiting for your meal. *40798 NW Logan Rd (at the north end of town, next to Safeway), Lincoln City, OR 97367; (541)996-3663; $; beer and wine; no credit cards; checks OK; breakfast, lunch every day, dinner Wed–Sun.*

DORY COVE

Appreciative crowds continue to flock to this place, rain or shine. Hearty American fare, Oregon Coast–style, is the theme here: lots of seafood, steak, tasty chowder, and 20-plus kinds of burgers (including a half-pound monster). Dessert centers around homemade pie à la mode. Road's End Wayside, a small state park with good clamming, is right next door. *5819 Logan Rd (next to state park), Lincoln City, OR 97367; (541)994-5180; $; beer and wine; AE, DIS, MC, V; checks OK; lunch, dinner every day.*

Smack dab in the midst of all the hubbub, Cafe Roma (1437 NW Highway 101; (541)994-6616) offers a sane haven with coffee drinks, Italian sodas, snacks, and reading material.

Roads End is a good clamming spot; tide tables are available at the nearby Dory Cove.

Tex-Mex? Try Hobie's Adobe (2733 NW Highway 101, (503)994-4419).

LODGINGS

INLET GARDEN OCEANVIEW BED AND BREAKFAST ☆

 Nestled on a steep hillside amid shore pines and dense shrubbery, Inlet Garden is an ideal alternative to Lincoln City's glitzy oceanfront lodgings. The house, originally belonging to John Gray (the developer of Salishan, a few miles to the south), is built in the Northwest regional style, with lots of windows and exposed wood and a sizable ocean-view deck (where Oregon wines and hot cider are served). Both bright and airy guest suites have private baths and fireplaces. The Azalea enjoys an engaging ocean view; the Manzanita features a private garden patio. Three-course breakfasts are memorable, and the beach is less than a quarter mile away. For those who'd rather be on the beach, consider renting the four-bedroom Backyard Beach house with stairs from the backyard right to the beach. *646 NW Inlet (¼ mile north of the D River Wayside), Lincoln City, OR 97367; (541)994-7932; fatcats@wcn.net; www.stylewise.com/oceanparadise; $$; AE, MC, V; checks OK.*

CAMP WESTWIND

 During June, July, and August, Camp Westwind, just south of Cascade Head and 5 miles north of Lincoln City, operates as a YWCA camp. The rest of the year, the 500-acre grounds are available for small or large groups. Small means no more than five in the Wy'East cabin, warmed by a stone fireplace and overlooking the mile or so of private beach; large means more than 40 in the main lodge, where a woodstove and a couple of fireplaces keep the cold at bay. Everyone must bring their own bedding, towels, and food. Don't plan on eating out, because you need to cross the Salmon River via barge just to reach the camp. No cars. *2353 N Three Rocks Rd, Otis, OR 97368; (541) 223-6281 (ask for camp programs); Reservations: YWCA, 1111 SW 10th Ave, Portland, OR 97205; $; MC, V; checks OK.*

GLENEDEN BEACH

The small unincorporated community of Gleneden Beach has grown up, primarily thanks to Salishan Lodge on Siletz Bay. The few restaurants are excellent, the beach is pristine, and the golfing is rated by Condé Nast *Traveler* as one of the Top 50 in the nation.

ACTIVITIES

Golf. Salishan's premier golf course is open to the public (though lodge guests receive a slight discount). It's 18 holes of world-class fun with half the course near the spit (some ocean views) and the other nine on the east side of the highway with more of an Oregon forest appeal; (800)890-0387.

Beautiful Homes. A 3-mile beach called the Salishan Spit protects the southern side of Siletz Bay. The beach is lined with some of Oregon's most expensive coastal houses, and vehicle access is restricted to property owners and guests. Because of Oregon's public beach law, however, everyone is allowed to hike the sand in front of the houses. The best access to Salishan Spit begins at Gleneden Beach State Wayside, a day-use park 1 mile south of Salishan Lodge on Hwy 101. Turn west on Laurel Rd and drive less than a mile to the large parking lot at the beach. Walk north 3 miles to the end of the spit. Another 3 miles of beach stretches south to Fogarty Creek State Park.

RESTAURANTS

CHEZ JEANNETTE ☆☆☆

Windows with flower boxes, whitewashed brick walls, and an intimate woodsy setting (as well as two fireplaces, usually blazing away in winter) give this establishment the appearance of a French country inn. The food is French—traditionally so— butter and cream are used in abundance, and most entrees are carefully sauced. And, bucking the seafood tradition seen up and down the coast, veal (sautéed medallions with a Dijon mustard sauce), roasted rack of lamb (with an Oregon pinot noir sauce), and pork (garnished with garlic, red wine, and juniper berries) make appearances on the menu. There's also a superb filet mignon and a nightly game selection (venison or, perhaps, duckling). But Chez Jeannette is by no means a slouch when it comes to seafood: Witness the baked Umpqua oysters, local mussels in a sumptuous saffron-cream sauce, and salmon poached in Triple Sec and served with a rhubarb compote. The escargots are the coast's finest. *7150 Old Hwy 101 (¼ mile south of Salishan Lodge on the old highway), Gleneden Beach, OR 97388; (541)764-3434; $$$; full bar; AE, MC, V; checks OK; dinner every day.*

SIDE DOOR CAFE

A pleasant new find on the coast well worth watching, this innovative restaurant in a renovated brick factory (although not a brick building) is giving its neighboring restaurants (Chez Jeannette and Salishan) a bit of a shakedown. Lunches are simple but savory (homemade soups, chicken wraps, and such). Chef David Shaefer (formerly of the Salishan) tosses up a tender rosemary-and-garlic-marinated lamb sirloin or a Thai coconut curry rock shrimp saute with Asian vegetables and jasmine rice with equal dexterity. A well-selected list of Oregon wines and microbrews and the Eden Hall Performance Theater make this a nice place to come, even if you're not hungry. *6675 Gleneden Beach Loop, Gleneden Beach, OR 97388; (541)764-3825; $$; full bar; MC, V; local checks only; lunch, dinner Wed–Sun.*

LODGINGS

SALISHAN LODGE   ★★★

Sprawled over a lush, green, 350-acre landscape, Salishan includes 205 guest rooms, arranged in 16-plex units that are nicely dispersed on a hillside rising from the main entrance. There's an 18-hole (par 72) golf course plus a driving range, 18-hole putting course, pro shop, and resident PGA professional. You can swim in a covered pool, play indoor or outdoor tennis, shoot some hoops at the outdoor basketball court, work out in the sizable fitness center, sweat in a sauna, or jog and hike the forested trails. Kids have their own game room. The huge wooden lodge, with vaulted ceilings and exposed beams, houses restaurants, a nightclub, a library, meeting rooms, and a gift shop. The guest units are spacious and tastefully furnished but not extravagant, with gas-fired fireplaces, view balconies (overlooking the forest, the links, or Siletz Bay), splashes of regional art, and individual carports. Forest, Sandpiper, and Overlook clusters, as well as both Chieftain Houses, benefit from secluded settings. Many unit clusters (including Tournament, Five Greens, Fairway, and the Sunset Suite) overlook the links; Tennis House is nearest the courts. As you'd expect, Northwest cuisine—alder-planked salmon, rack of lamb with a rhubarb-currant chutney, grilled abalone—dominates the menu in the main dining room, with its Siletz Bay views. The voluminous wine list represents a cellar stocked with 15,000 bottles, perhaps the region's foremost selection. Service throughout the resort is refined and purposeful (and less formal than previously). *On Hwy 101 in Gleneden Beach; (541)764-3600 or (800)452-2300; PO Box 118, Gleneden Beach, OR 97388; salishan@salishan.com; www.salishan. com; $$$; full bar; AE, DC, DIS, MC, V; checks OK; breakfast, lunch, dinner every day.*

Gracie's Sea Hag (Highway 101 in downtown Depoe Bay; (503)765-2734) is an institution around these parts, and a great place to catch up on the local scuttle-butt while downing a beer or mug of grog.

DEPOE BAY

Once a charming coastal community, Depoe Bay is now mostly an extension of Lincoln City's strip development. Fortunately, some of the original town, including its tiny harbor (billed as the "world's smallest"), remains intact.

ACTIVITIES

Bookworms. Channel Bookstore (Hwy 101, 1 block south of the bridge; (541)765-2352) is a used-book paradise filled with over 100,000 books and features everything from paperback romances to Latin grammar.

Gallery Hopping. The Harbor Gallery (211 SW Hwy 101; (541)765-3113) houses three floors of art. Amidst paintings, prints, and photographs of the Oregon Coast (and beyond), you'll find the living light gallery, where paintings change from day to night in an ultraviolet setting. The O'Connell Gallery (42 N Hwy 101; (541)765-3331) is more of a gift shop that features kinetic art (check out that gravitrain) and a great water-level view. Pat O'Connell likes eye-catching gadgets that thrill kids from 2 to 99.

Fishing Charters. For being the world's smallest harbor, Depoe Bay is home to some pretty big fishing. Offshore fishing here is very productive for salmon, halibut, and many species of rockfish. Prominent charter boat companies are Dockside Charters, (800)733-8915, and Tradewind Charters, (800)445-8730. Depoe Bay pumps out an average of 50,000 angler trips per year and the average catch is one of the highest on the Oregon Coast.

Searching for Spouts. Downtown Depoe Bay, right on the ocean, is a superb spot for storm- and whale-watching. Spectators can take a "saltwater shower" right along the seawall, courtesy of a blowhole located in the rocky ledge below—which blows regularly during winter sou'westers. When it gets really rough, the Pacific is, seemingly, ready to take over the town.

Whale Watching. Depoe Bay is a whale-watching mecca during the gray whale migratory season

(December to April). The leviathans may cruise within hailing distance of headlands, at times purposefully scraping off troublesome barnacles against offshore rocks. Watch for them at Boiler Bay Wayside (just north of town along Hwy 101), another spectacular storm-watching spot. Or head into whale territory. Deep Sea Trollers (downtown, adjacent to the harbor; (541)765-2248) is one of several operations offering whale-watching cruises.

 Scenic Views. Fogarty Creek State Park, 2 miles north of town, has a sheltered beach, well protected from coastal winds. There's an annual summer salmon barbecue held here; (541)765-2889. Come evening, the dramatic rock formations near the shore at Fogarty Creek nicely frame the sunsets and spew sea spray skyward at high tide. A mile farther north, Boiler Bay State Park offers dramatic cliffside photo ops and a good place to spot whales. The park was named for the remains of the *J. Marhoffer*, a small freighter that wrecked here in 1910.

There's a fabulous view from every table at Oceans Apart (177 NW Highway 101; (503)765-2513). At dusk, order a Hawaiian burger and stay for the daily light show. For a snack, try the Lincoln Beach Bagel Company (3930 Highway 101; (503)764-3882), a couple of miles north of town.

RESTAURANTS

TIDAL RAVES

 Indeed, diners rave about the imaginatively prepared seafood served in this enticing cliffside restaurant. Look for charbroiled Thai prawns, cornmeal-grilled snapper garnished with tomato relish, and penne pasta blended with sautéed scallops, feta, and sun-dried tomatoes. The extensive menu also lists lemon-rosemary chicken with polenta, oyster-spinach bisque, and broiled shrimp or crab sandwiches. Every table in the attractive interior overlooks sculpted cliffs, rock reefs, and crashing waves. Sunset raves, too. *279 NW Hwy 101 (on the west side of the highway), Depoe Bay, OR 97341; (541)765-2995; $$; beer and wine; MC, V; checks OK; lunch, dinner every day.*

LODGINGS

CHANNEL HOUSE

Intimate seaside inns (generally larger than B&Bs) with great settings and gracious service are gaining favor in the Northwest, and the Channel House was among the first. Spectacularly situated on a cliff overlooking the ocean and the Depoe Bay channel (literally right above the water, since there's no beach below), this place has 12 rooms, all with private baths, ocean views, and, come morning, a hearty breakfast. Ten units are truly special accommodations, outfitted with private decks, gas fireplaces, and spas (the seven roomier, and spendier, suites feature oceanfront spas on private decks). Two additional (and similarly appointed) suites are available in the owner's house, a few doors away. Whales might be sighted from your window; however, if you forgot your binoculars, no worry, you'll find a pair to borrow in every room. *35 Ellingson St (at the end of Ellingson St, above the ocean), Depoe Bay; (541)765-2140 or (800)447-2140; PO Box 56, Depoe Bay, OR 97341; cfinseth@newportnet.com; www.channelhouse.com; $$$; DIS, MC, V; checks OK.*

INN AT OTTER CREST ☆

 This rambling destination resort perched on 35 acres at Cape Foulweather is lushly landscaped with evergreens, coastal shrubs, and every color of rhododendron imaginable. Upon arrival, you leave your car and hop a shuttle van to your room, where traffic noise is nonexistent. Breathtaking views abound, but Cape Foulweather is aptly named: Summer fog often enshrouds the headland, though sunny skies may prevail just north and south. Still, most of the 280-plus units (not all are rentable, as some are privately owned) enjoy fireplaces, full kitchens, and superlative ocean vistas; all have private decks. Other amenities include an outdoor pool (with a sauna and spa) and tennis courts, along with volleyball, basketball, horseshoe, and shuffleboard areas. An isolated low-tide beach awaits 50 or so feet below, and nature trails lead to nearby Devil's Punch Bowl and additional beach access. *301 Otter Crest Loop (2 miles south of Depoe Bay), Otter Rock; (541)765-2111 or (800)452-2101; PO Box 50, Otter Rock, OR 97369; $$$; AE, DC, MC, V; no checks.*

NEWPORT

Newport's most popular former resident (Keiko the killer whale) has moved to a roomier sea-pen off the coast of Iceland; however, whale or no whale, Newport continues to be the most popular tourist destination on the Oregon Coast. And the relatively new Jazz on the Water Festival, held the last weekend in August at the Newport Marina, is creating just as big a splash in the music world. This superb three-year-old festival showcases world-class artists and Grammy-winning voices. The town itself continues to exhibit a blend of tasteful development (the Performing Arts Center, for example) with unending shopping center sprawl. The population is an eclectic mix, including crusty fishermen, artists, retirees, refuge-seeking yuppies, and counterculturists who never grew up. There's a wealth of variety in Newport; veer off Hwy 101's commercial chaos and discover what's here. The Nye Beach area, on the ocean side of Hwy 101, has fewer tourists and more of an arts-community feel.

When the ocean's too chilly—which is the case more often than not—there's a year-round, city-operated indoor pool in town (NW 12th; (503)265-7770).

ACTIVITIES

Aquarium. The pride of Newport—and the Oregon Coast—is the Oregon Coast Aquarium (2820 SE Ferry Slip Rd; (541)867-3474). It features furry, finny, and feathery creatures cavorting in re-created tide pools, cliffs, and caves. The main attraction now is the sea otters; other interesting animals include sea lions, seals, fish native to the Oregon Coast, and seabirds. The star of *Free Willy* departed for bigger digs in 1998.

Sea and Do. On the south side of the Yaquina Bay Bridge, Oregon State University's Hatfield Marine Science Center (2030 S Marine Science Drive; (541)867-0100) offers free marine-life displays, films, and field trips (including whale-watching excursions, which have an admission charge). Look into the summer Seatauqua program.

Fine Art. Oceanic Arts Center (444 SW Bay; (541)265-5963) and the Wood Gallery (818 SW Bay; (541)265-6843) are galleries worth visiting. The former offers jewelry, paintings, pottery, and sculpture; the latter, functional sculpture, woodwork, pottery, and weaving. The Newport Visual Arts Center

(839 NW Beach; (541)265-5133) displays traditional and radical art, and offers classes in an oceanfront setting.

Must Stop. Canyon Way Restaurant and Bookstore (1216 SW Canyon Way; (541)265-8319) boasts 20,000 titles, in addition to jewelry, lamps, rugs, and some great chow. Green Gables Bookstore (156 SW Coast St; (541)265-9141), in a restored older residence, has an interesting selection of women's and children's books. Independent travelers (and their well-behaved pets) like to stay in one of the two homelike rooms above the bookstore.

Views. Yaquina Bay, one of the busiest fishing spots on the Oregon Coast, meets the Pacific Ocean at Newport. Formed by the Yaquina River, the bay covers 1,700 acres and has tidewater inland for 13 miles. The south side of the bay is served by the Newport Marina at South Beach, (541)867-3321, a Port of Newport facility with a public boat launch at 2301 SE Marine Science Dr. One of the largest marine harbors on the Oregon Coast, the marina has 600 moorage slips, as well as parking for recreational vehicles and a complete line of support facilities. The city of Newport's bay front is a working waterfront going full tilt, where fishing boats of all types—trollers, trawlers, shrimpers, and crabbers—berth year-round. Park your vehicle, walk the waterfront, and soak up the salty ambience. For a bird's-eye perspective of boats, bay, and ocean, take a drive (or a walk) through Yaquina Beach State Park, which wraps around the south end of town.

Gone Fishin'. Many charter boat operators call the Newport bayfront home. Like their colleagues in other harbor towns along the coast, these folks lead salmon-, tuna-, halibut- and whale-watching excursions. Sea Gull Charters (343 SW Bay; (541)265-7441) and Newport Sportfishing (1000 SE Bay; (541)265-7558 or (800)828-8777) are two popular outfits. Beyond Fishing Marine Discovery Tours (345 SW Bay; (541)265-6200 or (800)903-2628) offers unusual saltwater excursions.

Beach Walks. There's plenty of beach to roam in these parts. Good access points include the Agate Beach area, just north of town, and Devil's Punch Bowl State Park, 8 miles north of Newport. Both spots include parking, rest rooms, and a trail to the beach. While you're at Devil's Punch Bowl, stop in for soup, espresso, or baked goods at the oceanfront Otter Rock Cafe (845 1st; (541)765-2628). Clamming and crabbing can be excellent in Yaquina Bay. Clam shovels and crabbing gear are available for rent at marine shops such as the Embarcadero Dock (on the bay front at 1000 SE Bay; (541)265-5435), which also rents boats.

State Parks. Four Oregon state parks offer camping near the beach in the Newport region. Each has campsites accessible to the handicapped and all but Washburne take reservations at (800)452-5687. The two most popular are the 130-acre Beverly Beach State Park, (541)265-4560, located 7 miles north of Newport, and the 434-acre South Beach State Park just west of Hwy 101 at the south entrance to Yaquina Bay. The other two parks with beach camping include the year-round but small Beachside State Park, (541)563-3220, and the 1,098-acre Washburne State Park, (541)997-3641, situated between two of the Oregon Coast's most photogenic headlands: Cape Perpetua to the north and Heceta Head to the south. Also ask about the availability of yurts at Beverly and South Beaches.

Explore the Bay. The Yaquina Head Outstanding Natural Area, (541)265-2863, is a 100-acre preserve situated at the north side of Agate Beach, 3 miles north of Hwy 101 (turn west on Lighthouse Dr). Besides fantastic cliff-front views, the Bureau of Land Management maintains several short interpretive trails on the peninsula, including the showcase Quarry Cove Tide Pools Trail. Dedicated in 1994, the quarter-mile-long trail was the world's first barrier-free path through a tide pool. The paved trail is under water during high tide, but when the tide goes out the sea life comes into view. Starfish, sea urchins, and sea cucumbers have slowly been moving back into the tide pool since its construction. The Yaquina Head Summit Trail (half a mile) gains 160 feet as it climbs to the top of the head from the east end of the parking loop. Yaquina Head Lighthouse at the tip of the cape is 93 feet high, and the tallest on the Oregon Coast. The lighthouse, which began operation in 1873, has daily tours during summer; call for a current schedule. The Yaquina Head Interpretive Center, which opened in 1997, sits on the site of an old gravel quarry.

Favorite galleries: Oceanic Arts and the Wood Gallery (both on the bay front), the Newport Visual Arts Center, the Back Porch Gallery in Yachats, and the Cannon Beach Arts Association Gallery.
—Sharon Morgan, executive director, Newport Performing Arts Center

Leave your dune buggy at home: Newport is at the heart of the longest vehicle-free strip of coast in Oregon.

Shopping Destination. Toledo, a mill town located 10 miles inland, is a wonderful side trip for antique and art lovers. Stop in at the Michael Gibbons Gallery (in the Vicarage at 140 NE Alder; (541)336-2797) and the Main Street Antique Mall (305 N Main; (541)336-3477).

Surf's Up. Surfing at Moolack Beach north of town is usually as good as it gets in Oregon. The surf's also often up at a number of area breaks. North to south, Devil's Punch Bowl, Beverly Beach, Agate Beach (especially just south of Yaquina Head), and the South Beach area, near the south jetty, all possess superior wave potential. The Punch Bowl is dangerous at high tide. The 1-mile trail that leads south from Otter Rock to Beverly Beach is popular with surfers and beach hikers. It's a long way to carry a surfboard but the waves are among the best in Oregon.

Festivals. For two weeks in July, classical musicians from throughout the country come to Newport to perform at the Ernest Bloch Music Festival (Bloch was a composer who lived in the Newport area). Call (541)265-ARTS for information. The Newport Seafood and Wine Festival is one of the oldest of its kind and the finest on the coast. Held in late February at the South Beach Marina, (800)262-7844, it draws from 15,000 to 20,000 people.

RESTAURANTS

CANYON WAY RESTAURANT
AND BOOKSTORE ☆☆

Canyon Way is as much an emporium as an eatery, with a bookstore, gift shop, deli, and restaurant on the premises. You could easily get sidetracked on the way to your table, or decide to forgo a sit-down meal in favor of the many take-out munchies available. If you stay, you'll find a pleasingly diverse menu loaded with seafood and fresh pasta plates. A Cajun turkey sandwich, grilled lingcod 'n' chips, and Dungeness crab cakes with angel hair onion rings, along with a variety of salads, are good noontime options. For dinner there's always a different baked oyster preparation daily, among other seafood selections. On sunny days, request an outdoor table overlooking the bay. *1216 SW Canyon Way (between Hurbert St and Bay Blvd), Newport, OR 97365; (541)265-8319; $$; full bar; AE, MC, V; checks OK; lunch Mon–Sat, dinner Tues–Sat (bookstore and deli open every day).*

WHALE'S TALE ☆

In tourist-oriented Newport, where mediocre restaurants come and go, the Whale's Tale has been serving up good food for more than 20 years. Unfortunately, the cavelike whale-motif interior looks ragged around the ribs, er, edges. Customers remain a healthy mix of fishermen, aging hippies, Newport yuppies, and adventuresome tourists. Breakfasts can be outstanding, with fresh jalapeño omelets, scrumptious poppyseed pancakes, and home-fried potatoes with onions and green chiles smothered in cheese. Lunches include good-sized sandwiches and a lusty fisherman's stew. A plate of grilled Yaquina oysters is a dinnertime favorite, along with lasagna, German sausage, ham and sauerkraut, and excellent black bread. *452 SW Bay Blvd (at Hurbert St), Newport, OR 97365; (541)265-8660; $$; beer and wine; AE, DC, DIS, MC, V; checks OK; breakfast, lunch, dinner every day (closed Wed in winter).*

COSMOS CAFE AND GALLERY

Deep-blue ceilings highlighted by heavenly bodies lend the Cosmos Cafe a spacey feel, but the grub and the prices are down to earth. You order from a serving counter, cafeteria-style, and then wait for your name to be called. The choices of salads, sandwiches, pastas, omelets, and Tex-Mex concoctions are legion. Try the Hawaiian ham-pineapple-and-onion sandwich wrapped in pita, the sassy Cajun-chicken burrito, or a hot pastrami on rye (a rarity for the coast). The adjacent Cosmos Gallery (same address; (541)265-4049) exhibits a diverse collection of pottery, oil paintings, stained glass, and furniture. *740 W Olive St (across from the Performing Arts Center), Newport, OR 97365; (541)265-7511; $; beer and wine; DIS, MC, V; local checks only; breakfast, lunch, dinner every day (closed Sun in winter).*

The Newport Performing Arts Center (777 S Olive; (503)265-ARTS) is an attractive wooden structure that hosts music, theater, and other events, some of national caliber.

Good pizza is tough to find on the coast. Try Don Petrie's Italian Food Co. (613 NW Third; (541)265-3663).

Long known for its chowder and fish 'n' chips, the original Mo's (622 SW Bay; (541)265-2979) is here. This Mo's offers a lot more of a briny atmosphere than its newer brethren, now scattered up and down the coast.

Fish Peddlers Market (617 Bay; (541)265-7057) is the source for fresh, smoked, and canned seafood.

LODGINGS

SYLVIA BEACH HOTEL ★★

 Owners Goody Cable and Sally Ford have dedicated their pleasantly funky bluff-top hotel to bookworms and their literary heroes and heroines. They gave several like-minded friends the task of decorating each of the 20 rooms, and the results are rich in whimsy and fresh, distinct personality—a true beach place, endearingly worn. Best way to do this hotel is to book (well in advance) one of the three "classics." The Agatha Christie Suite, for instance, is decorated in a lush green English chintz, with a tiled fireplace, a large deck facing out over the sea cliff below, and—best of all—clues from the writer's many murders. The "bestsellers" (views) and the "novels" (non-views) are quite small, not as impressive, but equally imaginative. Books and comfortable chairs abound in the library, where hot wine is served nightly at 10pm. Prepare for a stay sans phones, radios, TVs, and stress. Breakfast is included in the price of the room. Dinners in the hotel's Tables of Content restaurant are prix-fixe, reservation-only affairs. The main attraction is the company; the food (although it's noteworthy) gets secondary billing. *267 NW Cliff St (west on NW 3rd off Hwy 101, 6 blocks to NW Cliff), Newport, OR 97365; (541)265-5428; $$; beer and wine; AE, MC, V; checks OK; breakfast, dinner every day.*

NYE BEACH HOTEL AND CAFE ★

 There are so many lodging choices in Newport, it's fortuitous that two of the finest, and the most unusual, are virtually next door to each other. Just south of the Sylvia Beach Hotel, the newer Nye Beach Hotel and Cafe has a funky, '50s feel. Green metal railings lead to second and third floors, with narrow carpeted hallways sporting wildly shaped mirrors and myriad succulents. All 18 tidy guest rooms feature private baths, fireplaces, willow love seats, balconies, and ocean views. Six units have spas. The hotel's lobby, awash in eclectic tunes, has a piano and a tiny bar. Steps lead down to a bistrolike setting where a suave waitstaff serves an equally eclectic dinner (but you'll often find Mexican offerings and the requisite clam chowder). Outside, there's a large and heated deck for oceanfront dining. *219 NW Cliff St (just south of the Sylvia Beach Hotel), Newport, OR 97365; (541)265-3334; www.teleport.com/~nyebeach/hotel.html; $$; full bar; AE, DIS, MC, V; checks OK; breakfast, lunch, dinner every day.*

OCEAN HOUSE ☆

Roomier and slightly less quaint than its former incarnation, the Ocean House affords some privacy in the Oregon Coast's most bustling area. Host Bob Garrard is the epitome of congeniality, and the setting remains picture-perfect—overlooking the surf at Agate Beach, with Yaquina Head and its lighthouse towering nearby. The five guest rooms, all with private baths and ocean views (and some with spas), are homey and comfortable—neither elegant nor luxurious. There's a small library with cushy chairs and a roaring fireplace in the winter. Outside, you can enjoy a full breakfast on sunny mornings or just relax and sunbathe, protected from the summer northwest wind in the sheltered backyard and garden. A short trail leads to the beach below. If Ocean House is booked, consider the Tyee Lodge (with five guest rooms) across the street and also oceanfront. *4920 NW Woody Way (just off Hwy 101 N in Agate Beach, 1 block south of Yaquina Head Lighthouse Rd), Newport, OR 97365; (541)265-6158 or (800)56BANDB; $$$; MC, V; checks OK.*

Head to Yaquina Head (follow the signs to the Outstanding Natural Area) or Cape Foulweather, 9 miles north of Newport (which, unfortunately for sun worshippers, often lives up to its name), to view the sunset.

THE VIKINGS

These rustic 75-year-old cottages occupy an oceanfront bluff, while a steep but sturdy staircase leads to an untrampled beach below. All 13 cottages have color TVs; some have fireplaces and kitchens. Off-season rates begin at $50. Designed for couples, the romantic, wood-paneled Crow's Nest (room 10) is a second-story studio with a double bed, kitchen, private bath with shower, and an unbeatable Pacific panorama (and prices that creep just beyond our bargain range during the summer season). *729 NW Coast St, Newport, OR 97365; (541)265-2477 or (800)480-2477; $; AE, DC, MC, V; checks OK.*

SEAL ROCK

Recently artists and others seeking more elbow room have moved here from crowded Newport. It's still not much more than a patch of strip-development along Hwy 101, but within that patch are a few keepers, including Yuzen (the best Japanese restaurant along the entire coast) and the 8-acre state wayside at Driftwood Beach along Hwy 101 (one of the best views).

ACTIVITIES

Recreation. Beaver Creek winds its way through Ona Beach State Park (a mile north of town), providing fishing, swimming, and bird-watching possibilities. A footbridge takes you to a little-used beach. On the south end of Seal Rock, a state park of the same name features a rocky intertidal area perfect for viewing (look, but don't touch!) starfish, sea anemones, and other marine life. Catch a glimpse of a sunbathing seal at the small but picturesque Seal Rock Wayside. Another quick stop for a stunning click is Driftwood Beach Wayside, 4 miles south of Seal Rock.

Coastal Birds. A portion of the Oregon Islands National Wildlife Refuge is located offshore from the central coast. Gull, Whaleback, Yaquina Head, and Otter Rocks are all offshore north of Newport, while Seal Rocks are located 4 miles north of Waldport. The 575 acres of the coastal refuge system encompass 1,400 offshore rocks, islands, and reefs and are home to large numbers of seabirds and marine mammals. It's illegal to set foot on the islands, but their animal life can be seen through binoculars from highway pullouts the length of the Oregon Coast.

Local Art. Some interesting chain-saw art is being created at Seal Rock Woodworks (along Hwy 101; (541)563-2452). Art on the Rocks (5667 NW Pacific Coast Hwy, 2 miles north of the Alsea Bay Bridge; (541)563-3920) has paintings, carvings, crafts, and jewelry.

River Run. The Alsea River is one of the most heavily boated medium-size rivers along the Oregon Coast. The lower river is busy with fishermen in drift boats, especially during winter when the river's main run of steelhead is present and during fall when chinook are running. Boat landings are numerous along the river and can be used for launching canoes and sea kayaks for trips to the bay. The Alsea River also offers a 32-mile float, with Class I and occasionally Class II rapids, from the Mill Creek Park launch 2 miles west of Alsea on Hwy 34 in Benton County downstream to the town of Tidewater, 10 miles east of Waldport.

RESTAURANTS

YUZEN ★

You may think you're hallucinating. A Japanese restaurant residing in a Bavarian-styled building, located in Seal Rock, a blink of a town with a Wild West motif? No, Yuzen is for real—the home of the coast's finest Japanese cuisine. Even if raw fish isn't your idea of a delectable morsel, you'll enjoy the mildly flavored tuna, salmon, and prawn served in the sushi sampler appetizer (which you should order anyway, as it may take a while for your entree to arrive). Sukiyaki is splendid, as are the tempura dishes. Dinners include a decent miso soup and a small salad. There's even a *wafu* steak, a traditional Japanese grilled New York steak with two sauces and veggies. And if you've never tried sake or matcha (green tea) ice cream, this is the place. *Hwy 101 (8 miles south of Newport), Seal Rock, OR 97394; (541)563-4766; $$; beer and wine; MC, V; checks OK; lunch, dinner Tues–Sun.*

Take the scenic 9-mile drive east of Waldport to the Kozy Kove (9464 Alsea Highway 34, Tidewater; (541)528-3251), a restaurant and lounge afloat on the Alsea River.

WALDPORT

Small, quiet, unpretentious Waldport is situated on the wide and lovely Alsea River estuary, where Hwy 101 makes a big bend to accommodate its sandy shore. There are untrampled beaches at either end of town, and a city center unspoiled by schlock. At the south end of the Alsea Bay Bridge (rebuilt in 1991) is an interpretive center with historic transportation displays.

ACTIVITIES

Alsea's Bounty. Surf-casting and rock fishing are popular at the west end of Alsea Bay. The Alsea River, home to salmon, steelhead, and sea-run cutthroat trout, is suitable for virtually any type of angling. The Waldport Salmon Derby is held each fall. Phone the Chamber of Commerce, (541)563-2133, for dates and information. Clamming and crabbing are excellent in Alsea Bay. The Dock of the Bay Marina (1245 Mill; (541)563-2003) rents all you'll need, including boats.

Special Spots. Tillicum Beach Campground, operated by the Forest Service, is 4 miles south of Waldport along Hwy 101. It's a perfect picnic spot with beach access. Park yourself on Yaquina John Point, at the end of Adahi Rd (just south of town and adjacent to the Cliff House Bed and Breakfast). There's a breathtaking view of bay and ocean, complete with barking seals. One of the pristine stretches of the Coast Range, the remote, pocket-size Drift Creek Wilderness, accessible only by foot or on horseback, is tucked into the range halfway between Seal Rock and Waldport; Waldport Ranger District, 1049 SW Pacific Coast Hwy; (541)563-3211.

LODGINGS

CAPE COD COTTAGES ☆

Between Waldport and Yachats, the beach becomes narrower and less frequented. Cape Cod Cottages, sitting on a low bank just off Hwy 101, occupies 300 feet of this ocean frontage, with easy beach access. Ten cozy (and spic-and-span) one- and two-bedroom units come with fully equipped kitchens, fireplaces (with wood provided), decks, and picture windows overlooking the ocean. The larger units sleep as many as eight. Some even have garages. All in all, this is a nice, out-of-the-way place where children are welcome. *4150 SW Pacific Coast Hwy (2½ miles south of Waldport, on Hwy 101), Waldport, OR 97394; (541)563-2106; $$; AE, DIS, MC, V; checks OK.*

Waldport is the home of Inkfish Magazine, the best source of information for central coast happenings. You can pick it up at any coffee shop or market in town.

CLIFF HOUSE BED AND BREAKFAST ☆

 At this bright blue B&B perched atop the Alsea River's mouth, you can watch seals and salmon-hungry sea lions just below, as well as migrating whales and memorable sunsets. Four ultraposh rooms are available; all include antique furnishings, chandeliers, color TVs, water views, and balcony overlooks. The Bridal Suite (the price is no honeymoon) houses a tufted-velvet sleigh bed with canopy, an oceanfront mirrored bath with Jacuzzi, and a shower for two. That said, we've withheld a star due to numerous reports of uneven service (a vital component of any B&B), but our anonymous spies continue to claim they've witnessed nothing less than top-notch attention. Out back, there's an ocean-view deck with an oversize spa, as well as a sauna and steam room, croquet course, and a hammock for two. Massages can be had in the cliff-side gazebo (or in your room) for a fee. Obviously, no children or pets. *1450 Adahi Rd (1 block west of Hwy 101), Waldport; (541)563-2506; PO Box 436, Waldport, OR 97394; clifhos@pioneer.net; www.virtualcities.com; $$$; MC, V; checks OK.*

EDGEWATER COTTAGES ☆

 Although not isolated, the Edgewater is located 2½ miles south of town on an oceanfront bluff with easy beach access. All seven cottages feature attractive wood interiors, ocean-facing sun decks, fireplaces, TVs, and kitchens, but no phones. Larger families should rent the Rustic, a two-bedroom affair that sleeps six. Alas, there are some strings attached (a four-night minimum stay in the summer; no one-night reservations any time of the year), but the hassles are worth wading through. Be sure to call in advance (for your pet, too), and leave your credit card at home. The cute, pint-size Wheel House (a steal at $65) is strictly a two-person affair, while the Beachcomber can accommodate as many as 15 guests. The owners live on premises, contributing to the homey atmosphere. Pets okay for a small additional fee. *3978 SW Pacific Coast Hwy (2½ miles south of Waldport, on Hwy 101), Waldport, OR 97394; (541)563-2240; $$; no credit cards; checks (in advance) OK.*

SOUTHERN OREGON COAST

Along large sections of the southern Oregon Coast, life goes on the way it always has—slowly. Here, miles of untouched shoreline far outnumber fast-paced commercial strips. From Yachats south to the California border, only a few towns of any size break up the 160-mile stretch of mostly wild seashore. A long succession of state parks and 50 miles of the Oregon Dunes National Recreation Area ensure that this paradise will not be subjected to the over-development that has ravaged sections of the northern coast.

Small tribes of Native American hunter-gatherers first settled along this coast more than 5,000 years ago. European contact began in the late 16th century when, most historians believe, English mariner Sir Francis Drake sailed as far north as the Oregon Dunes area and became the first non-native to lay eyes on the northwest coast of North America. In his wake came other European and American seafarers led, initially, by the Spanish. Capes Ferrelo, Sebastian, and Blanco, as well as Heceta Head, are geographical reminders of these explorers' maritime forays to this area.

The Columbia River, and the Strait of Juan de Fuca farther north, became the focal points for further exploration and subsequent settlement, while the south coast remained relatively undisturbed. Perhaps because of this isolation, the folks who live here now are fiercely independent. With the exception of the stretch between Yachats and Coos Bay (a one-day, round-trip drive from Eugene), the south coast is a long way from any urban center; it remains a wild place with a singular sense of openness.

YACHATS

Yachats (pronounced *YAH-hots)* takes its name from a Chinook Indian word meaning "dark waters at the foot of the mountain," which fits this small community's setting on a narrow basaltic terrace straddling the Yachats River. Paths lead down from seaside bluffs to beaches and rocky tide pools at the state park and across the river mouth at Yachats Ocean Wayside. The beach in Yachats is rocky and rife with tide pools and whooshing geysers. Yachats itself is another hip, Cannon Beach–type arts community with an interesting mix of aging counterculturists, yuppies, and tourists. It's also a prime area for harvesting sea-run smelt (savory sardinelike fish that congregate near the shore during mating season, May through September).

ACTIVITIES

Galleries. Favorite galleries include Earthworks Gallery (2222 N Hwy 101; (541)547-4300), which exhibits Northwest artists, the Backporch Gallery (4th and Hwy 101; (541)547-4500), and the Tole Tree (2334 Hwy 101; (541)547-3608).

Trails with a View. South of Yachats, the 2,780-acre Cape Perpetua Scenic Area embraces one of the most spectacular sections of the Siuslaw National Forest. The namesake cape, a prominent basaltic headland, towers 800 feet over the coast. At the foot of the cape, heavily visited Devil's Churn is a narrow fissure where frothing seawater surges in and out. Cape Perpetua Scenic Area, (541)547-3289, also contains the highest concentration of hiking trails along the Oregon Coast. The visitors center is 2.6 miles south of Yachats on the east side of Hwy 101. Trails are rugged but climb to spectacular viewpoints. Coast access is available on the Trail of Restless Waters (half a mile) and the Captain Cook Trail (half a mile), both just off Hwy 101. The 2.6-mile round-trip St. Perpetua Trail (which begins at the Cape Perpetua Visitors Center) climbs 600 feet to the West Shelter, a stone hut on the brow of the cape that on a clear day takes in an extraordinary 150-mile panorama up and down the coast, from Cape Foulweather down to Cape Blanco. It's also a fine aerie for spying whales passing far below. There are numerous other trails (shorter and longer), and the visitors center (2400 Hwy 101 S), where trail maps are available, is a good starting point. Cape Perpetua is one of the wettest regions on the Oregon Coast; the cape's summit gets well over 100 inches of rain annually. If you hike the trails, particularly in the backcountry, bring rain gear; even when it's clear and sunny to the north or south, you may see moisture here.

Orca Whilefoods (84 Beach Avenue, Yachats; (541)547-4065) sells tempting salads and fresh-squeezed juices.

More Hiking. Those in search of a tamer hike should head for the Yachats 804 Trail, which begins at the Smelt Sands Wayside at the north end of town and winds its way along the ocean bluffs. This is national forest territory, crisscrossed with hiking trails that lead to isolated coves. The driftwood-strewn beaches and rocky ledges are often bombarded by monstrous ocean waves. Other paths head deep into bona fide rain forest (with 400 tons of plant life per acre) and into the Cummins Creek Wilderness Area.

Sealife. One half mile south of Cape Perpetua is Strawberry Hill, an easily missed picnic area where wild strawberry plants flower in the spring. Throughout the year, harbor seals lounge like plump gray slugs on the rock shelf 30 yards offshore. April, May, and June are the prime months to look for their newborn pups, which weigh about 20 pounds. The rocky coastal fringe here forms some of the best tide pools, alive with swaying sea anemones, sea urchins, scuttling hermit crabs, periwinkles, and a miniature world of other intertidal sea organisms. Up above, spectacular headlands afford ocean-viewing or whale-watching promontories.

Sea Lions. Though at first they appear along the highway like a misplaced Disney sideshow, the Sea Lions Caves (91560 Hwy 101; (541)547-3111; $5.50 per adult), 11 miles north of Florence, are nevertheless one of the central coast's most impressive natural phenomena, the only place on the U.S. mainland where Steller's sea lions can be seen year-round. And it's much less kitschy than all the advance hype might suggest. (Can 200,000 visitors a year possibly be wrong?) An elevator carries you 208 feet down into the vast, surf-swept cavern, where the booming of the waves mingles eerily with the tenor barking of the sea lion bulls. As your eyes adjust to the gloom, you'll see the sea lions frolicking or dozing on the rocks, some within arm's

*For fine views, drive
the aptly named
Auto Tour View-
point Road
(off Highway 101,
3 miles south of
Yachats), a switch-
backed blacktop
that winds its way
up Cape Perpetua.
Trails leading from
the parking area
on top provide
sweeping vistas.*

reach. They occupy the cave during the fall and winter; in spring and summer they give birth to their young just outside the cave.

Biking. The Yachats River Rd (at the south end of town) is a little-used paved route that heads into an undeveloped area of the Coast Range. It's a spectacular 19-mile loop via bike or car through the pastoral Yachats River Valley and up into old-growth in the Suislaw National Forest. A shorter (but just as hilly) bike route begins at Cape Perpetua and continues south through the National Forest. Trail riders should pick up a map of the Cummins Vista mountain bike loop from the Cape Perpetua Visitors Center (2400 Hwy 101 S; (541)547-3289).

Photo Opportunity. The next large headland to the south is Heceta Head, named for 18th-century Spanish navigator Bruno Heceta. Heceta Head Lighthouse is the Oregon Coast's most powerful—and popular—beacon. The darling of lighthouse buffs, it's said to be the most photographed on the West Coast; however, it's not open to the public. From April through August, look for colonies of Brandt's cormorants, which nest on the rugged south slope.

RESTAURANTS

LA SERRE ☆

Fine dining options drop off drastically south of Newport, but La Serre ("the greenhouse") is one of the central coast's better restaurants. The largest plant collection this side of Cape Perpetua's rain forest highlights a dining area with overhead skylights and a beamed ceiling. Herbal aromas redolent of garlic and saffron drift down from the open kitchen, while an appealing (and roaring in winter) fireplace distinguishes an adjacent lounge. Seafood is a good bet, be it catch-of-the-day Pacific whitefish, Umpqua oysters, or zesty cioppino; vegetarian dishes are top-drawer, too. *160 W 2nd (2nd and Beach, downtown), Yachats, OR 97498; (541)547-3420; $$; full bar; AE, MC, V; local checks only; dinner Wed–Mon (closed Jan).*

NEW MORNING COFFEEHOUSE ☆

A crosssection of Yachats society—hip locals in Gore-Tex and jeans, Eugene weekenders, and tourists—visits this pleasant roadside respite. They come for superb muffins, pies, and coffee cakes, as well as black bean chili and omelets. The congregation huddles around the homey woodstove in winter; in warm weather, folks head for the out-of-the-wind back porch to partake of evening pasta specials. *373 Hwy 101 N (at 4th St), Yachats, OR 97498; (541)547-3848; $; beer and wine; DIS, MC, V; checks OK; breakfast, lunch every day, dinner Thurs–Sat (closed Mon–Tues in winter).*

The colorful Yachats Kite Festival lifts off during blustery October (usually the first Saturday), when the winds grow strong enough to float kites as big as Oldsmobiles; (503)547-3530.

LODGINGS

SEA QUEST BED AND BREAKFAST ★★

Few B&Bs on the Oregon Coast are better situated than this (well, the Ziggurat next door, perhaps). At Sea Quest you spend the night in a luxurious, estatelike structure located on a sandy, beach-grassed bluff right above the ocean and nearby Tenmile Creek. Four out of the five guest rooms have spas in their baths, plush queen-size beds, private entrances, and ocean views. Miles of Pacific vistas are yours to enjoy from the spacious living room. Scan the horizon with the spyglass, or plunk down with a good book in one of the commodious chairs. *95354 Hwy 101 (6½ miles south of Yachats on west side of Hwy 101, between mile markers 171 and 172), Yachats; (541)547-3782 or (800)341-4878; PO Box 448, Yachats, OR 97498; www.seaq.com; $$$; MC, V; checks OK.*

ZIGGURAT BED AND BREAKFAST ★★

This stunning, four-story glass-and-wood structure takes its name from the Sumerian word for "terraced pyramid." It sits on a sandy knoll, up against the roaring Pacific and the gurgling waters of Tenmile Creek. Scintillating views from all 40 windows keep most guests occupied, especially during storms (the glass-enclosed decks are ideal); however, there are also plenty of books and board games in the

2,000-square-foot living room. The east suite boasts a sauna, while the west suite has a round, glass-block shower and a magnificent view. If you're in the market for a quality B&B, this just might be your place. *95330 Hwy 101 (6½ miles south of Yachats on west side of Hwy 101), Yachats; (541)547-3925; PO Box 757, Yachats, OR 97498; $$$; no credit cards; checks OK.*

THE ADOBE RESORT ☆

 Ensconced in a private, parklike setting, the Adobe fans out around the edge of a basalt-bumpy shore. At high tide, waves crash onto the rocks below while their thunder echoes through the building. The rooms are sizable and come with refrigerators, TVs, VCRs, and coffeemakers. Most have ocean views and a number have fireplaces. The plusher suites (some with spas and fireplaces) all look out on the ocean. All guests have access to a six-person Jacuzzi and sauna. Children are welcome, and pets are allowed in the northwest wing and the four-person apartment units. The on-site restaurant, as oceanfront as you can get (every table enjoys a water vista), rates a notch above the usual mediocre beachtown fare. *1555 Hwy 101 (downtown), Yachats; (541)547-3141 or (800)522-3623; PO Box 219, Yachats, OR 97498; $$; full bar; AE, DC, DIS, MC, V; checks OK; brunch Sun, breakfast, lunch Mon–Sat, dinner every day.*

BURD'S NEST INN BED AND BREAKFAST ☆

 This is one distinctive roost, perched halfway up a hillside and enjoying a big bird's-eye view of the Pacific. The half-century-old home has a cluttered but comfortable look, especially inside, where antiques, unusual toys, and knickknacks compete for wall and table space. The proprietors lend an animated, friendly ambience and specialize in made-to-order breakfasts. *664 Yachats River Rd (east side of Hwy 101, just before the bridge), Yachats, OR 97498; (541)547-3683; $$; MC, V; no checks.*

THE SEE VUE

 Perched cliffside between Cape Perpetua and Heceta Head, the See Vue lives up to its name with miles of

Pacific panoramas. Each of the 10 units in this cedar-shake lodging is differently appointed. The Salish, with its Northwest Native American motif, offers the sweetest deal. Other rooms are decorated with different themes (such as the Mountain Shores, with its redwood burls, and the second-story-view Crow's Nest, with nautical furnishings). Most rooms are less than $65. Your hosts can fill you in on the goings-on in Yachats and Florence, or you may prefer to meander down to the uncrowded beach a few hundred yards away. *95590 Hwy 101 S, Yachats, OR 97498; (541)547-3227; $; MC, V; checks OK.*

SHAMROCK LODGETTES

Disregard the cutesy name; these rustic log-cabin-like units, sequestered on a grassy, 4-acre oceanfront terrace with easy beach access, are cozy and comfortable. All 19 "lodgettes" (some are cabins, but most are rooms) enjoy fireplaces, while some have small kitchens. Rooms 8 through 15 and apartment 7 are the best deals. Cabin 6, with two bedrooms and baths, sleeps eight. A separate structure houses a sauna and spa open to all guests, and personal massages can be arranged. Pets are welcome in the cabin units. *On Hwy 101 S (just south of the Yachats River bridge), Yachats; (541)546-3312 or (800)845-5028; PO Box 346, Yachats, OR 97498; shamrock@netbridge.net; $$; AE, DC, M, V; checks OK.*

WAYSIDE LODGE

No doubt about it: This unpretentious (and extremely accommodating) lodging located a few miles north of Yachats is one of the coast's sweetest deals. Three low-lying, ocean-blue buildings are nestled in a thicket of shore pines, nicely sheltered from Hwy 101. All seven recently spruced-up units have a well-equipped kitchen, TV, secluded deck, and ocean view. There's a grassy area out back just above the beach, and even though houses sit on either side, a feeling of privacy prevails. The screamin' deal here is Cottage 1, a single-story studio with easy beach access ($55 in season). *5773 N Hwy 101, Yachats, OR 97498; (541)547-3450; $; DIS, MC, V; checks OK.*

The lounge at the Adobe Resort (1555 Highway 101; (541)547-3141) is as oceanfront as you can get. The food's nothing to write home about, but the view is definitely worth the price of a drink or brew.

Favorite outdoor spots: Cape Perpetua and Strawberry Hill beach, a little way south, where there are lots of agates and marine life.
—Donald Niskanen, co-owner, New Morning Coffeehouse

FLORENCE

The once sleepy lumber and fishing port of Florence, the northern gateway to the Oregon Dunes National Recreation Area, is now a vibrant tourist mecca. The tastefully revitalized Old Town has become decidedly visitor-oriented—with cafes, gift shops, and a movie house concentrated along riverside Bay Street—without succumbing to the schlock that afflicts other parts of the Oregon Coast.

ACTIVITIES

Miles of Dunes. The real attraction on this stretch of coast is the 47-mile-long Oregon Dunes National Recreation Area, 32,000 acres of mountainous sand dunes, freshwater lakes, beaches, and marsh. Stretching almost 50 miles from Florence to North Bend, the extraordinary national recreation area was established by Congress for its scientific and historic value as well as for recreation and conservation. Because from the highway you can only glimpse this sandy wilderness, plan to stop and explore on foot. Good starting points near Florence include the Cleawox Lake area of Honeyman Memorial State Park and the Tahkenitch Lake area a few miles farther south. The best day-use facilities in the Oregon Dunes accessible by automobiles for picnicking, kite flying, or beachcombing are located along 4 miles of South Jetty Rd that run along the beach to its end at the south jetty of the Siuslaw River in Florence, or along the 2.5 miles of road that dead-end in the dunes south of the Umpqua River in Reedsport. The Oregon Dunes National Recreation Area's headquarters is located in Reedsport (855 Hwy 101; (541)271-3611).

Motorized Fun. The Oregon Dunes National Recreation Area stretches for 47 miles along the coast, from the south jetty of the Siuslaw River near Florence to the Horsfall area at the north end of Coos Bay. The dunes vary in width from 1 to 2 miles. Because of the dry, shifting sand, much of the dunes lacks paved roads and walking can be very difficult. As such, an off-road vehicle can be the best way to cover the territory and become intimately familiar with the dunes. While most of the dunes are open throughout the year to vehicles, some portions have summer closures and other parts are closed permanently. Although most closed areas are signed, it's the driver's responsibility to know where riding is allowed around the three major staging areas: North Siltcoos, High Dunes, and South Dunes. Four-wheel all-terrain vehicles—dune buggies—rent for $20 for a half hour, up to $175 for the day; however there are lots of hidden charges such as damages, rescues, cleanup, and deposits, so compare prices, be safe, and have fun. A few rental places include Sandland Adventures of Florence, (541)997-8087; Dune Odyssey of Winchester Bay, (541)271-3863; and Winchester Bay Rentals of Winchester Bay, (541)271-9357.

The Oregon Dunes are the nation's largest coastal sand dunes.

Dune Tours. For those who just want to see the dunes, guided tours in large passenger vehicles may be the way to go. Escorted tours, as well as vehicle rentals, are offered by San Dunes Frontier and Theme Park of Florence, (541)997-3544; Dune Buggy Adventures of Winchester Bay, (541)271-6972; Pacific Coast Recreation of North Bend, (541)756-7183; and Spinreel Dune Buggy Rentals of North Bend, (541)759-3313. Tours start as low as $10.

Pitch Your Tent. To camp at the Oregon Dunes National Recreation Area, choose from 14 U.S. Forest Service campgrounds; of these, eight allow off-road vehicles. For reservations, call (800)280-2267. The majority are nestled amid the dunes; some are near a river or lake. Tyee River, Carter Lake, and Tahkenitch Lake have boat ramps; Tahkenitch Campground, Eel Creek, and Spinreel offer picnicking; Spinreel and Horsfall have staging areas for off-road vehicles; Driftwood, Taylor, Tahkenitch Campground, Spinreel, and Horsfall are wheelchair-accessible; Spinreel, Wild Mare, and Horsfall have horse-staging lots; and hiking opportunities are plentiful at all. None of the campgrounds have hookups, and a 10-day stay is usually the maximum. For a free guide to the hiking opportunities, stop by the Oregon Dunes headquarters on the west side of Hwy 101 at the intersection of Hwy 38; (541)271-3611.

Hiking. Walking in the sand can be quite tiring, so be conservative on the length of hike you choose. Three of our favorite dune hikes include the Oregon Dunes Overlook Trail, 10 miles south of Florence (3.5 miles round trip; difficult) and the

Locals head out South Jetty Road, south of Florence on Highway 101, for miles of broad, sandy beach and pounding surf, plus high dunes zoned for use by off-road vehicles.

Tahkenitch Creek Trail, 11 miles south of Florence, where there are three moderate, separate loop trails of 1.5, 2.5, and 4 miles. The third, the Umpqua Dunes Trail (a moderately difficult 3 miles round trip) in the southern dunes between Reedsport and North Bend, leads through the Umpqua Scenic Dunes (primarily off-limits to motor vehicles).This trail begins at the Eel Creek Campground 10.5 miles south of Reedsport on Hwy 101.

Mush, You Huskies! The Oregon Dunes Mushers Mail Run, held since 1977, is a one-of-a-kind event—a dogsled race with a twist, held not on snowy tundra but across miles of sand dunes and forest trails. The world's longest dry-land run, it spans the length of the dunes from Horsfall Beach in the south to the dunes west of Florence.

Two classes of teams participate, using specially designed four-wheel sleds: mini-teams consist of 3 or 4 dogs and cover 55 miles; traditional teams of 5 to 12 dogs traverse the whole grueling 72 miles. Proceeds from the run, held the second weekend in March from 7am to dusk, go to support an Oregon competitor in Alaska's famed Iditarod Trail Sled Dog Race. Before the run, you can buy souvenir envelopes commemorating the route at the Florence and North Bend Chambers of Commerce; the envelopes are hand-canceled at the post offices, carried on the sleds during the race, and signed by the driver. Afterward, all the teams gather for a parade and other festivities in Old Town Florence. Go down to the beach in any of the areas between Florence and Coos Bay; head to Lakeside in the late afternoon on Saturday to see the mini-teams, and to Winchester Bay on Sunday morning to see the start of the final stretch. For more information, call the Bay Area Chamber of Commerce at (800)824-8486 or the Florence Visitors Center at (541)997-3128.

A Sternwheeler Cruise. The 65-foot *Westward Ho* (PO Box 3023, Florence, OR 97439; (541)997-9691), a modern replica of an 1850s sternwheeler, moored at the Bay Street dock in Old Town, cruises up the Siuslaw River to Mapleton and back. "The Rockin' 'n' Rollin'" on the River tour (Saturdays 1pm to 3pm) includes live music, card and board games, old-time photos, beer, wine, and a gourmet salmon brunch ($20 for the cruise; $13 for the brunch; kids under 13 for $10). The Time Warp Cruise (Sundays 1pm to 3pm) features a narrated "living history" cruise. Enjoy complimentary champagne with brunch while taking in the tidal river and wildlife scenery.

The Oregon Coast's annual rainfall is 55 to 80 inches, the bulk of which accumulates in the winter.

Botanical Wayside. The Darlingtonia Botanical Wayside, 4 miles north of Florence just off Hwy 101, protects 18 boggy acres where the unusual carnivorous pitcher plant *(Darlingtonia californica)* thrives. To compensate for the nitrogen-poor wetland soil, the plants feed on insects, which are lured by scent and nectar into the flaring stem. Once inside, the victims become trapped and are eventually digested. The pitcher plants, shaped something like a snake's head (hence another nickname—the cobra lily), bloom in May and June, but can be seen here throughout most of the year; a quarter-mile loop trail leads through the wooded preserve for a close look.

Dune Birding. More than 240 species of birds have been sighted in the Oregon Dunes, with 130 species present during practically any time of the year. For a copy of a bird checklist, stop at the Oregon Dunes National Recreation Area headquarters, (541)271-3611, at 855 Hwy Ave in Reedsport. Rather than the seabirds the coast is famous for, the dunes harbor herons, grouse, woodpeckers, warblers, and finches. It pays to keep a bird book and binoculars handy. Shorebirds are easy to spot, however, south of the Siuslaw River's South Jetty. At the end of South Jetty Rd is a fishing/crabbing pier near the jetties; while you fish, watch hundreds of wintering tundra swans, with their 6-foot wingspans, that inhabit the wetlands from mid-November to February.

Horseback Riding. The busiest beach of all for horseback riding is Baker Beach. Weekend cowboys tow their trailers to the equestrian trailhead and set up camp. Or you can rent your steed from C&M Stables (90241 Hwy 101 N, Florence, OR 97439; (541)997-7540), 8 miles north of Florence on Hwy 101, which offers horseback journeys that let riders of all abilities explore secluded ocean beaches and forests of the Coast Range. Guided beach rides of 1½ ($23) and 2 hours ($28) leave the ranch on a trail that winds through scenic dunes and onto the beach; sunset rides last 2 hours. You may even ride all day. Reservations are highly recommended. Large groups can be accommodated, especially in summer.

Camping. Harbor Vista Park near the north jetty of the Siuslaw River in Florence is one of the few coastal campgrounds with an ocean view; (541)997-5987. Jessie M. Honeyman Memorial State Park, 3 miles south of Florence on Hwy 101, is one of the most beloved in the Oregon parks system because the campground offers swimming and fishing in Cleawox Lake, plus waterskiing across the highway in Woahink Lake; (541)997-3641, or call (800)452-5687 for reservations.

RESTAURANTS

INTERNATIONAL C-FOOD MARKET

 "Catch it, cook it fresh, and keep it simple" is the plan at this sprawling seafood operation right on the Siuslaw River pier at the edge of Old Town. The fish-receiving station and the fleet are just outside the restaurant, and it's fun to watch the boats unload (a sign explains what kind of seafood), then order a fillet prepared just the way you want it. There are crab, oysters, and clams, too. Visit the attached seafood market for fresh take-out. *1498 Bay St (at the Siuslaw River), Florence, OR 97439; (541)997-9646; $$; full bar; MC, V; checks OK; lunch, dinner every day.*

LODGINGS

COAST HOUSE ★★

To call this place picturesque, exclusive, or even spectacular might be understating the case. Coast House is certainly one of a kind, and it's rented to only one group (one or two couples) at a time. The location couldn't be finer—total seclusion on a forested (1½-acre) oceanfront cliff just south of Sea Lion Caves. But you'd never find it on your own, so you need to rendezvous with owners Nancy Archer and Ron Hogeland in Florence beforehand. The four-level, 1,000-square-foot structure features two sleeping lofts with skylights, a full kitchen, roomy living quarters, and a bath with a claw-footed tub overlooking the ocean. Electric baseboard heat keeps

Coast House warm, and an antique wood-burning stove (ample fuel provided) renders it romantic. All necessities (robes, music, a bottle of wine) except food are provided, but there is no phone or TV. Kids and pets are taboo. *10 miles north of Florence (call for details); (541)997-7888; PO Box 930, Florence; $$$; no credit cards; checks OK.*

JOHNSON HOUSE BED AND BREAKFAST ★★

We can't recommend any hotels in Florence, so we're thankful for the wit, curiosity, and lofty aesthetic standards Jayne and Ron Fraese bring to their perennially popular B&B. Reflecting the Fraeses' interests (he's a political science prof, she's an English teacher), the library is strong on local history, natural history, politics, and collections of essays, letters, cartoons, and poetry. There are six guest rooms, one of which is a cute garden cottage. Breakfasts, which include fresh garden fruit and produce (grown out back) and home-baked bread, are among the best on the coast. The Fraeses live next door, so they're available to assist guests. They also own Moonset, an extraordinary, couples-only lodging north of town (2 miles south of Sea Lion Caves). This spendy ($250 a day) retreat includes a CD library, full kitchen (stocked with staples plus a complimentary bottle of Oregon wine), sauna, and a sizable, ocean-view spa. *216 Maple St (1 block north of the river in Old Town), Florence; (541)997-8000 or (800)768-9488; PO Box 1892, Florence, OR 97439; fraese@pesys.com; $$; MC, DIS, V; checks OK.*

EDWIN K BED AND BREAKFAST ★

Built in 1914 by one of Florence's founders, the Edwin K is set in a quiet residential neighborhood beyond the bustle of Old Town. Inside, the place looks formal but feels warm and homey. Ivory wall-to-wall carpeting contrasts nicely with aged and swarthy Douglas fir woodwork. All six spacious guest rooms are fitted with private baths and adorned with antiques and crystal. Breakfast is served in the exquisitely appointed dining room, another shrine to the woodcrafter's art. Out back, there's a private

Yurts—rigid-walled, domed tents with electricity, bunks, tables—can be found in eight coastal parks (all you need is a sleeping bag and a reservation). North to south, they are Fort Stevens, Nehalem Bay, Cape Lookout, Beverly Beach, South Beach, Jessie M. Honeyman, Bullards Beach, and Harris Beach. They usually run about $27.50 per night for up to five campers (most can sleep more) with an extra charge for additional campers.

courtyard with a 30-foot waterfall. *1155 Bay St (on the west edge of Old Town, across the street from the river), Florence; (541)997-8360 or (800)8EDWINK; PO Box 2686, Florence, OR 97439; $$; MC, DIS, V; checks OK.*

OCEAN HAVEN

 Ocean Haven (formerly known as Gull Haven Lodge) offers a setting—high on a cliff overlooking the charging Pacific—that is perhaps as close to perfect as any lodging on the Oregon Coast. A 360-degree panorama is available from the Shag's Nest ($90), an isolated one-room cabin equipped with a fireplace, kitchen, and private deck (you'll need to book it well in advance). The lodge units aren't as good a deal, though two cedar-lined sleeping rooms with ocean views, which share a bath and a kitchen, are a bargain at $40. With binoculars in each room and tide pools out the door, this is a wonderful stopover for the curious explorer. *94770 Hwy 101, Yachats, OR 97498; (541)547-3583; $; MC, V; checks OK.*

REEDSPORT

The faded logging center of Reedsport hasn't yet fully discovered its potential and personality on the Hwy 101 stretch, midway between Florence and Coos Bay. But this port town of 5,000 on the Umpqua River is the center for information on the dunes, and the wharf area is undergoing revitalization.

ACTIVITIES

Fishing. The Umpqua River is renowned among anglers for its spring chinook run and fighting steelhead; shad runs spring and summer, and sturgeon and striped bass are taken from the lower stretches.

A Crab Hunt. One of the more offbeat events on the central coast is the Kleo the Krab Bounty Hunt. This local family favorite runs from mid-August though Labor Day. Several score live crabs are tagged and released into the harbor, then the public is invited to catch them (supplying their own crab pots and other equipment). Participants win T-shirts and other prizes. To the lucky crabber who lands Kleo goes a hefty $1,000; if Kleo hasn't been nabbed by Labor Day, a winner is chosen by lottery. For more details, contact the Lower Umpqua Chamber of Commerce (PO Box 11, Reedsport, OR 97467; (541)271-3495 or (800)247-2155).

Museum. Located wharfside on the Umpqua River, a half mile east of Hwy 101, the Umpqua Discovery Center (409 Riverfront Way, Reedsport, OR 97467; (541)271-4816) opened in mid-1993 and features two main exhibits. The "Umpqua Experience" examines the region's human and natural history. Admission to all exhibits is $3 for adults, $1.50 for kids 5–12.

Wildlife Viewing. Three miles east of Reedsport, the Dean Creek Elk Viewing Area is a 1,040-acre preserve alongside the Umpqua River. It is a wildlife-rich mosaic of wetlands, pasture, and forest. Top billing, of course, goes to the herd of 60 to 100 Roosevelt elk, the largest species of elk in the world. Males can weigh in at over 700 pounds, bearing massive racks; females are smaller and lack antlers. Both have thick dark fur around the neck and shoulder area that help distinguish them

The well-informed staff makes the Oregon Dunes National Recreation Area Headquarters (855 Highway Ave, Reedsport, OR 97467; (541)271-3611) a useful stop for tips on hiking trails and on where to go to spot elk, ospreys, and other wildlife.

from deer. The majestic elk are year-round residents, but they're often scarce; they usually emerge from the sheltering woods at dawn and dusk. Sections of the wetlands have been enhanced to provide more standing water for a variety of wildlife. Canada geese winter here and nest on the pastures. Along streambanks and marsh edges, look for nutria, dog-size rodents that resemble beavers, but with ratlike tails. Introduced from South America around 1900 for the fur market, the nutria quickly adapted—too well—and rapidly spread throughout much of the United States. Keep your eyes open for less conspicuous creatures, too: rough-skinned newts, garter snakes, frogs, and other reptiles and amphibians. Other residents and seasonal visitors at Dean Creek include western bluebirds, black-tailed deer, ospreys, great blue herons, and mallard ducks. Binoculars will definitely come in handy here. For more information, contact the Bureau of Land Management (1300 Airport Lane, North Bend, OR 97459; (541)756-0100) or stop by the National Recreation Area information center in Reedsport.

WINCHESTER BAY

Four miles southwest of Reedsport down Hwy 101 at Winchester Bay is the Salmon Harbor Marina and its thicket of commercial and private boats; with nearly a thousand slips, this is the largest sport-fishing marina on the Oregon Coast.

ACTIVITIES

Fishing. Winchester Bay and the Umpqua River estuary comprise one of Oregon's most diverse fisheries, combining offshore angling for salmon, halibut, and bottom fish with outstanding bay fishing year-round for nearly all of Oregon's fish species. The bay is also good for clams and crabs. Some of the world's tastiest oysters come from commercial beds located in a triangle formed by jetties off the mouth of the Umpqua. One of the largest marinas on the West Coast, Salmon Harbor Marina, located in Winchester Bay, is home to charter boats that offer fishing and whale-watching trips; call the marina at (541)271-3407 for information on charters. Several outfits are based here, including Gee Gee Charters, (503)271-3152 or (503)271-4134, which runs bottom-fish and Chinook expeditions. And when you return to port, bone tired but full of good stories (and, hopefully, your limit), you'll find several salmon canneries and smokehouses to process your haul.

Lakes. With 32 lakes, the Oregon Dunes National Recreation Area attracts more fishermen than off-road vehicle riders. The dunes are lined by all types of lakes, from the 3,000 acres covered by Siltcoos Lake to the famous clear waters of 82-acre Cleawox Lake in Honeyman State Park. Siltcoos Lake, 6 miles south of Florence on Hwy 101, is one of Oregon's best warm-water fisheries (bass, bluegill, trout, yellow perch, crappie, and bullhead). Tenmile and North Tenmile Lakes, interconnected twin lakes formed when Coast Range streams were dammed by sand dunes, attract anglers (for bluegill and large-mouth bass), swimmers, water-skiers, and canoeists, all of whom can explore the many arms. Located east of Lakeside (Hwy 101) and northeast of Oregon Dunes National Recreation Area.

"People love lighthouses. There are five working lighthouses in Oregon and there's even a national and a statewide lighthouse organization whose members act as lighthouse tour guides. On the first weekend we opened, we ran tours up the Umpqua Lighthouse. Five hundred-and-eighty people went through it in a day and a half... five people at a time."
—Frank Marshall, Umpqua River Lighthouse tour guide

Motorized Fun. Spinreel Dune Buggy Rentals (9122 Wildwood Dr, North Bend, OR 97459; (541)759-3313), about 2 miles south of Tenmile Lakes (look for mile marker 224), rents Odyssey dune buggies ($30 per hour, $155 all day) and other off-road vehicles. You can take a spin along the beach or putter up and down the dunes. Phone ahead in winter.

Thar She Blows! The grounds of the Umpqua River Lighthouse (built in 1894) in Umpqua Lighthouse State Park offer a prime whale-watching perch, 100 feet above sea level, anytime. From Alaska's Bering and Chukchi Seas, pregnant gray whales begin passing the Oregon Coast in late November—usually averaging one whale per hour—on their 12,000-mile maternity run to the warmer waters off Baja, California. In late December the main pulse arrives, when one whale may swim past every two minutes or so. From March to May they make their way north again. Call ahead about the daily tours of the still-working lighthouse; (541)271-4631.

Doing the Dunes. If you've got time for just one jaunt into the dunes, the Umpqua Dunes Trail, an easy, 4-mile round trip, is a prime candidate, taking you into some of the highest dunes and far from the sputter of off-road vehicles. From Eel Creek Campground, about seven miles south of Winchester Bay, follow the foot trail west. After a quarter-mile climb through a forest of evergreens and rhododendrons, you'll break through the tree line and step out onto some of the most impressive dunes in all of this miniature Sahara, cresting nearly 500 feet high. After about another mile across the sand, you reach the "deflation plain," a low-lying marshy area that's gradually being reclaimed by pine forest. Deer and other animals can be spotted here, as well as a variety of native plants, including the insectivorous sundew. Follow the blue-banded poles marking the route for another three-quarters of a mile to the beach. (A shorter alternative: Join ranger-led groups on the Eel Creek Dunes Trail, a 1-mile loop, leaving the Eel Creek Campground Wednesdays at 2pm, late June through August.)

NORTH BEND

Across Highway 101 from Horsfall Beach, Clausen Oysters (811 N Bay Drive, on Haynes Inlet; (541)756-3600) is the place to buy oysters.

Near the southern end of the dune country, North Bend, Coos Bay, and Charleston—collectively dubbed the "bay area"—combine to form the largest urban area on the Oregon Coast. North Bend began in the mid-1800s as a company town where sea captain and shipbuilder Asa Simpson established a sawmill and shipyard. Though the town was in a rugged coastal frontier, replete with saloons and houses of ill repute, it was picturesque and prosperous enough to attract newcomers as highways and railways were erected nearby. Today's North Benders bear a striking resemblance to the early settlers—a population of solid working folk, retirees, and the occasional new face. Many folks drive through without stopping. North of town, just before the bay bridge, is the turnoff to Horsfall Beach and the southernmost access to the Oregon Dunes Recreation Area.

ACTIVITIES

Jazz Fest. In mid-March, North Bend and Coos Bay pump up the volume with a three-day jazz festival, held annually since 1988: the South Coast Dixieland Clambake Jazz Festival (PO Box 374, North Bend, OR 97459; (541)756-4613). More than a dozen bands play at four venues around the area (connected by a shuttle), with a program comprised mainly of classic or old-style jazz (an over-40 crowd usually prevails). Tickets are about $40 for all three days. The Sunday morning gospel service is free.

Biking Routes. Two scenic detours away from Hwy 101 make pedaling the 31 miles of the Oregon Coast Bike Route from North Bend to Bandon one of the most interesting sections of the 368-mile route. Learn more about the Cape Arago Hwy/Seven Devils Rd (26.7 miles) and Beach Loop Rd (17.5 miles) detours at Moe's Bicycle Shop in North Bend; (541)756-7536. A side trip through Charleston on the Cape Arago Hwy leads to many of the area's most scenic destinations (see Charleston, below).

LODGINGS

HIGHLANDS BED AND BREAKFAST ☆

It's the secluded, woodsy setting and the view of the Coast Range and Coos Bay that lure people to these 6 acres of highlands. Then there's the comfortable 2,000-square-foot lower level of Marilyn and Jim Dow's contemporary cedar home. A commodious living room with a soapstone stove and wraparound windows is at your disposal, as is a private solarium deck with a spa. If you want to try your hand at crabbing, the Dows will loan you their crab ring and cook whatever good creatures you net. No children under 10. *Please call for directions; 608 Ridge Rd, North Bend, OR 97459; (541) 756-0300; $$; MC, V; checks OK.*

COOS BAY

The south bay's port city and formerly the world's foremost wood-products exporter, Coos Bay has been undercut by a sagging timber industry and the political struggle to control the future of the Northwest's forests. But this Scandinavian/German-founded town still has the largest and busiest natural harbor between San Francisco and Seattle.

And that's the impression visitors get as they enter the town along Hwy 101—steaming mills and industrial areas, with few of the bells and whistles that induce highway cruisers to pull over and linger. Much of the downtown's architecture and businesses look unchanged from the 1950s. But frankly, that's part of Coos Bay's rough-around-the-edges charm. The town is, however, making the slow transition from a resource-based economy to one that's service-based, and that means catering—albeit grudgingly—to tourism. The downtown wharf area, for example, is being spruced up, with informative displays on Coos Bay's maritime and timber history (including a dry-docked tugboat), and there is a lovely art museum (see below).

"I don't like oysters, but I've got one guy out here, if he gets hungry out in the field, he'll stop, pick one up, shuck it, and pop it in his mouth. I've seen oysters here that are 8 to 12 inches across— big as a guy's forearm. I found an oyster that had the start of seven little pearls all in a nine-inch shell."
—Stacy Heathcock, manager of an oyster harvesting crew

ACTIVITIES

Fine Art. Coos Art Museum (235 Anderson St, Coos Bay, OR 97420; (541)267-3901) is the biggest surprise in this burly mill town—the only coastal art museum between San Francisco and Vancouver, British Columbia. The centerpiece of local cultural efforts, the museum, with 3,500 square feet of exhibit space, is housed in the art deco former post office building in central downtown. The impressive permanent collection features American prints, oils, watercolors, and sculpture, and includes works by Larry Rivers, Robert Rauschenberg, and James Rosenquist. The Mabel Hansen Gallery and Oregon Gallery usually spotlight works by up-and-coming artists. One of the most popular annual events is the "Public Hanging," an unjuried exhibit held in autumn showcasing artists from around Oregon. The museum is a venue for dance and music performances, and also sponsors classes and workshops in various art media. The first-floor gift shop carries contemporary art and handcrafts—limited-edition prints, ceramics, jewelry—from around the Pacific Northwest. Open most afternoons. Admission is by donation.

Myrtlewood. Travelers soon learn that the Oregon bay area is myrtlewood country. From the numerous crafts shops that specialize in myrtlewood gifts to the trees themselves, this famous hardwood is never far from sight. An evergreen and the only tree of the genus *Umbellaria*, it belongs to the laurel family and produces tiny yellow flowers in late winter. The wood is highly prized for carvings and used for everything from grandfather clocks to tacky souvenirs. The Coquille Myrtle Grove, 14 miles south of Myrtle Point off Hwy 42, has a picnic area set amid a lovely stand of old myrtlewood trees along the Coquille River. A brochure entitled "Discovering Oregon's Evergreen Hardwood" is available from local chambers of commerce to guide visitors to 28 public groves, from the Umpqua River to the California border. You can also buy your own at the House of Myrtlewood (1125 S First Street, Coos Bay; (541)267-7804 or (800)255-5318) where there's a free 20-minute tour of the myrtlewood factory (see woodturners, carvers, and nishers in action).

Water Music. The Oregon Coast Music Festival (Box 663, Coos Bay, OR 97420; (541)267-0938) gathers an impressively heady roster of American and international performers for concerts in Reedsport, Coos Bay/North Bend, and Bandon. The eclectic series, held over the second half of July, includes just about everything from baroque to folk, spiced with jazz, Broadway show tunes, and chamber and orchestral works. Past highlights have included brass ensemble concerts en plein air in the lovely gardens at Shore Acres State Park, and organ recitals on the vintage Wurlitzer in Coos Bay's classic Egyptian Theatre. Series passes are available; some events are free.

RESTAURANTS

BLUE HERON BISTRO   ☆☆☆

A European-style bistro in downtown Coos Bay, where longshoremen and timber workers still hold sway, may seem unlikely; but the Blue Heron keeps customers happy with an airy atmosphere, indoor and alfresco dining, and a reasonably priced, innovative menu. There are waffles, breakfast parfaits, and strong jolts of java in the morning. Other times, look for handcrafted pastas, blackened oysters, a German sausage plate, and grilled salmon with black beans, corn relish, and salsa. Desserts are top-drawer and so are the more than 40 varieties of bottled beer. *100 W Commercial (Hwy 101 and Commercial), Coos Bay, OR 97420; (541)267-3933; $$; beer and wine; MC, V; local checks only; breakfast, lunch, dinner every day.*

KUM-YON'S ☆

Believe it: This nondescript eatery is a showcase of South Korean cuisine. Some Japanese (sushi, sashimi) and Chinese (eggflower soup, fried rice, chow mein) dishes are offered, but to discover what really makes this place special, you'll have to venture into the unknown. Try spicy hot *chap chae* (transparent noodles pan-fried with veggies and beef), *bulgogi* (thinly sliced sirloin marinated in honey and spices), or *yakitori* (Japanese-style shish kabob). Get there early on weekends. Or check out the Kum-Yon's in Newport *(1006 SW Coast Hwy; (541)265-5330). 835 S Broadway (at the south end of the main drag), Coos Bay, OR 97420; (541)269-2662; $; beer and wine; AE, DIS, MC, V; local checks only; lunch, dinner every day.*

BANK BREWING COMPANY

A bank turned microbrewery, this inviting downtown establishment features a congenial pub atmosphere with high ceilings, huge windows, and balcony seating. Sweet Wheat and Gold Coast Golden Ale top the craft-beer list, while enticing chow choices include calamari, stuffed jalapeños, mussels, clams, and hand-tossed pizzas. *201 Central Ave (corner of 2nd), Coos Bay, OR 97420; (541)267-0963; $; beer, wine; MC, V; checks OK; lunch, dinner Mon–Sat.*

LODGINGS

COOS BAY MANOR BED AND BREAKFAST ☆

Head up the hill away from the commercial glitz of Hwy 101 and you'll discover beautifully restored homes among deciduous and coniferous trees and flowering shrubs. The Coos Bay Manor, a grand neocolonial-style structure with large rooms and high ceilings, is such a place, located on a quiet residential street overlooking the waterfront. An open-air balcony porch is situated upstairs, where Patricia Williams serves breakfast on mellow summer mornings. The five guest rooms (three with private baths) are all distinctively decorated (the Baron's Room is decked out with marble walls and a four-poster canopy bed; the Victorian features lace and ruffles). Mannerly children and dogs who tolerate cats are welcome. *955 S 5th St (4 blocks above the waterfront), Coos Bay, OR 97420; (541)269-1224 or (800)269-1224; $$; MC, DIS, V; checks OK.*

BLACKBERRY INN

The Blackberry Inn offers a different twist on the usual B&B arrangement. Guests here have the renovated 1903 Victorian home to themselves; the owners have their own residence. Breakfast is a continental affair, but a kitchen is available, and eggs and bread are supplied. There are four guest rooms; two have private baths. A night in the small but adequate Rose Room is a genuine bargain ($60 summers; $50 off-season), especially in urbanized Coos Bay. Centrally located, the inn is within walking distance of most of downtown. Unfortunately, it fronts a busy thoroughfare. *843 Central Ave, Coos Bay, OR 97420; (541)267-6951 or (800)500-4657; $; MC, V; checks OK.*

CHARLESTON

For an exhilarating side trip and gorgeous sunsets, get off Hwy 101 and head west about 10 miles on the Cape Arago Hwy to Charleston and beyond, back to the wildly beautiful shore. Charleston is the third-largest commercial port on the coast, as the piscatorial scent in the air reveals; industry here includes fish-processing plants for tuna, salmon, oysters, and shrimp. Not surprisingly, it's a great place to find some of the tastiest seafood dishes anywhere on the coast, or pick up fresh picnic and barbecue fixings on your way to the nearby state parks.

The Wasson Creek Trail, down Seven Devils Road from the South Slough estuary reserve, is just three-quarters of a mile, with moderate-to-easy walking through meadow and forest. Songbirds, birds of prey, elk, beaver, and deer frequent the area. Allow 45 minutes.

ACTIVITIES

Oysters. Qualman Oyster Farms (4898 Crown Point Rd; (541)888-3145), in business since 1937, is the largest producer of oysters on the south Oregon Coast. With 235 acres of oyster beds, it produces up to 6,000 gallons of bluepoint oysters per year. These "stick-grown" oysters are more easily harvested than traditionally raised oysters and are quickly transferred for shucking. Stick-growing produces larger (as big as your hand), cleaner shellfish; about $4 a dozen. Qualman Farms is just a few miles south of Coos Bay; follow signs from Cape Arago Hwy. Open Monday through Saturday.

Town Tanks. The harborside Oregon Institute of Marine Biology, headquartered here, is not open to visitors, but in summer it does set up a public display near the boat basin, with interpretive exhibits and tanks filled with various live sea creatures. Late May through September. Call for more information: (541)888-2581.

Paddler's Paradise. South Slough National Estuarine Research Reserve (PO Box 5417, Charleston, OR 97420; (541)888-5558) protects 4,500 acres of tidal habitat, salt marshes, mudflats, and woodlands set aside for research, education, and recreation. Hiking, bird-watching, and canoeing are the most popular activities. At the reserve interpretive center, get maps, directions, and personal guides. Learn to plan around the tides: With the tide's cooperation, the 4-mile-long slough is a two-hour paddle in either direction.

Open every day in summer, weekdays only from Labor Day to Memorial Day.

Nature Trail. The Estuary Study Trail in the South Slough National Estuarine Research Reserve (see above) is a 3-mile round-trip walk, beginning at the center. Descending 300 feet on a graded hill, it follows Hidden Creek down to the slough, where habitats change from forest to swamp and marsh. At the bottom of the marsh, a lookout is set up for viewing indigenous birdlife. Allow two hours for the hike.

Warm Waters. Sunset Bay State Park, 11.5 west of Coos Bay along the Cape Arago Highway; (541)888-4902) has a pretty, vest-pocket cove hemmed in by 50-foot cliffs—a good spot to dip your feet or take a swim, especially for kids. With a palisade of rocks guarding its seaward side, the cove is perpetually calm, even during midwinter sou'westers, when a colossal surf rages a couple of hundred yards offshore. It's also some of the warmest coastal swimming waters you'll find in Oregon. Day use is free. There is a grassy picnic and year-round camping area nearby, as well as a public golf course.

Lumber Baron's Estate. Shore Acres State Park (13030 Cape Arago Hwy, Charleston, OR 97420; (541)888-3732) is a thousand-acre coastal gem and the former estate of lumber and shipping baron Louis J. Simpson. His original summer home grew over the years into a mansion with an indoor pool and elaborately landscaped grounds. The home burned down in 1921 and was replaced, but by the 1940s all the property had been donated or sold to the state of Oregon. Unable to maintain Simpson's former home, the state razed it in 1948. What remains are the gardener's cottage (the second mansion's former dining-room wing), formal gardens, and breathtaking cliff-edge views. The beautifully maintained botanical gardens include a Japanese lily pond, rose gardens, a greenhouse, and exotic plantings from around the world. Several trails run through the forested property, leading along the clifftops and down to a secluded little cove.

From the viewing gazebo perched atop a dramatic bluff, you can watch the storms piling up offshore. On either side, the layered sedimentary rocks have been carved into almost organic patterns and formations. Tilted upward, they face the furious swells like a ship's prow, sending white fountains of spray some 80 feet into the air. Admission to the park is free. It's open during daylight hours year-round.

Bluff Views. Cape Arago State Park, located at the end of the road 1 mile south of Shore Acres, covers 134 acres on top of the 200-foot-high coastal bluff. Picnic tables are spread among openings in the thick coastal forest. A paved path leads down to the beach of North Cove, while a trail takes you to tide pools at South Cove. The Oregon Coast Trail winds along the cliff tops here and connects with Shore Acres and Sunset Bay State Parks. Cape Arago overlooks the Oregon Islands National Wildlife Refuge, home to birds, seals, and sea lions, so bring binoculars. But don't expect to view the Cape Arago Lighthouse from here; it can best be seen offshore from a scenic wayside a couple miles north along Cape Arago Hwy.

RESTAURANTS

PORTSIDE ☆

It's dark and cavernous inside, so you'll notice the lighted glass tanks containing live crabs and lobsters—a good sign that the kitchen is concerned with fresh ingredients. From your table, you can watch fishing gear being repaired and vessels coming and going in the Charleston Boat Basin. Naturally, fresh seafood that is simply prepared is the house specialty. For something different, try the "cucumber boat," a medley of shrimp, crab, and smoked salmon accompanied by cucumber dressing. Fridays there's a seafood buffet that includes everything but the anchor. *8001 Kingfisher Rd (just over the Charleston bridge, in the midst of the boat basin), Charleston, OR 97420; (541)888-5544; $$; full bar; AE, DC, MC, V; local checks only; lunch, dinner every day.*

One of the south coast's best bookstores is Winter River Books (170 Second Street; (541)347-4111). This Old Town bookstore is a light, inviting place, with a balanced selection of literature, travel, new age, health, and art books, and CDs.

BANDON AND CAPE BLANCO

A self-proclaimed storm-watching hot spot and cranberry capital, Bandon looks—and feels—newly painted, freshly scrubbed, and friendly. Some locals believe that Bandon rests on a "ley line," an underground crystalline structure reputed to be the focus of powerful cosmic energies. Maybe so. What's certain is that, as one of the most developed and thriving of the coast's "old towns," Bandon's magnetism does seem to lure visitors right off the adjacent highway to stroll around the shops, galleries, and cafes of its compact center. Wind-hammered Cape Blanco, with its 1870 lighthouse, is the most westerly point in the Lower 48. Furious Pacific Ocean storms, making their first landfall here, seem to take this fact personally, and they pummel Cape Blanco with all their might: winds here have been clocked at over 180 miles per hour.

ACTIVITIES

Cranberries. The naturally acidic, peaty soil of this area has proved ideal for raising cranberries, and Bandon has almost 1,000 acres under cultivation. The September Cranberry Festival, a 50-year tradition, pays tribute to the town's foremost fruit. Four days of community celebration include an arts and crafts show, float parades through Old Town, kite-flying contests, the crowning of the Cranberry Queen, tours of the cranberry bogs, and a food fair, in which competitors vie to create the most imaginative cranberry dishes. Good old-fashioned fun; contact Bandon Chamber of Commerce for specific dates; (541)347-9616.

Sweet Things. Stop in at locally renowned Cranberry Sweets (501 1st St; (541)347-9475), where they concoct such delectables as cranberry truffles, candy, fudge, and other treats. They ship all over, and their confections have even caught the attention of the *New York Times*. The staff is friendly, and very generous with samples. Open daily. The cranberry jam at the family-run Misty Meadows roadside stand (Hwy 101 south of Bandon; (541)347-2575) is a perennial favorite, too. The family has been producing coveted jellies, jams, and syrups for a quarter of a century, and is reportedly the oldest cottage industry in the state.

Cheese Tour. Though less well known than its larger counterpart in Tillamook, Bandon's Cheddar Cheese Factory (Hwy 101, just north of Bandon; (800)548-8961) is worth a stop to see cheese being made by hand, as it has been for over a century, at one of the last of the many cheese plants that once thrived along the coast. The Bandon plant's history began during the 1880s, when fresh milk was transported by stern-wheeler. The "full cream cheddar," made from whole Jersey milk, soon became sought after for its rich flavor. Today, they still age some varieties of cheese up to 24 months. In addition to several cheddars, they also produce Monterey Jack, Colby, and flavored cheeses; samples available.

Boice-Cope County Park is the site of the large freshwater Floras Lake, popular with boaters, anglers, and board sailors. An extensive trail network invites hiking and mountain biking (take the hike to isolated Blacklock Point).

Fish Food. Budget gourmets will appreciate the inexpensive "walk-away" seafood cocktails at the Bandon Fisheries Market (250 SW 1st at Chicago; (541)347-2851). They make for a quick, tasty meal to munch at harborside tables. Other delicacies here include smoked trout and salmon, shrimp, and crab.

Beachcombing. A good place for exploring is Bullards Beach State Park, 1 mile north of Bandon on Hwy 101; (541)347-2209. This gem of a park occupies an expansive 1,266 acres cross-cut with hiking and biking trails that lead to uncrowded driftwood- and kelp-cluttered beaches. The park has big grassy areas for kite flying, year-round camping (192 sites total), and good windsurfing beaches on both the river and ocean sides of the park. The 1896 Coquille River Lighthouse is a beauty, located across the dunes at the end of the park's main road. The tower is not open to the public, but the attached main building, with informational plaques and great views of the Coquille River mouth, is.

Horseback Riding. Bullards Beach State Park also has one of the best horse camps of the coast state parks, with corrals and two horse trails that lead from camp to the beach. Experience Bandon's beach on horseback with Bandon Beach Riding Stables (2640 Beach Loop Dr; (541)347-3423).

Sand Sculpture. Bandon's annual Sandcastle/Sandsculpture Contest (Ray Kelley, PO Box 335, Bandon, OR 97411; (541)347-2511), held on Memorial Day, is always a big hit. Individuals and teams, from preschool age and up, compete for prizes and, if not their 15 minutes of fame, then at least the sort that lasts till high tide comes in. Starts in early morning, on the beach at Seabird Lane and Beach Loop Road.

Seabirds. Coquille Point Wildlife Park was recently designated a wildlife park to protect the nesting seabird colonies on the adjacent rocks, part of the Oregon Islands National Wildlife Refuge. Six acres of weather-beaten coastal headland have been reshaped, layered with topsoil, and planted with native vegetation. There is a newly developed wheelchair-accessible pedestrian trail that winds past interpretive information on nesting seabirds (murres, guillemots, tufted puffins, and others), marine mammals, bird migration, and the Coquille Estuary. For information, contact Shoreline Education for Awareness (SEA) (PO Box 957, Bandon, OR 97411; (541)347-3683). SEA members can be found in the point parking lot fielding questions every Saturday morning from midspring to late summer.

More Birds. Bandon Marsh National Wildlife Refuge (half a mile north of Bandon; (541)757-7236), is a 289-acre refuge with some excellent shorebird sitings, including a Mongolian plover and a sharp-tailed sandpiper. Harbor seals are seen frequently inside the sandbar.

Lions, Tigers, and Bears. You don't expect to find snow leopards and Siberian lynx on the southern Oregon Coast, but the West Coast Game Park (Rte 1, Box 1330, Bandon, OR 97411; (541)347-3106), 7 miles south of Bandon on Hwy 101, is home to these big cats and another 75 domestic and exotic animal species. At the country's largest wild animal petting park, you'll also see lions, tigers, bears, cougars, antelope, peacocks, monkeys, camels, bison, zebras—some 450 birds and animals in all—on 26 wooded acres. Be prepared for a closer encounter than you'll get at most zoos. Adult animals pace back and forth in large viewing pens (scrutinizing you just as much as you do them), but their offspring are available for petting. To accustom them to human contact, public relations director

Debbie Tramell says, animals are hand-raised by park employees. "They even take the animals home with them at night for feeding purposes. Lion cubs need to be bottle-fed every two hours," Tramell says. Once the young animals mature beyond petting age, some are moved to zoos; others are trained for stage and screen. Open daily March through November, weather permitting. Winter hours vary.

I Spy. Around Bandon, as elsewhere in Coos County, coastal headlands are good places to watch for the offshore parade of wildlife that inhabits the islands and reefs of the Oregon Islands National Wildlife Refuge system. While public entry to the offshore islands is prohibited, a good pair of binoculars and a spotting scope help bring the impressive seabird colonies—including tufted puffins—into easy view. Tide pools can be found at Sunset Bay and Cape Arago State Parks (see Charleston, above), Five-Mile Point off Seven Devils Rd, and Coquille Point on the west edge of Bandon. Designated California gray whale-watching sites are at Shore Acres State Park near Charleston, Face Rock Wayside at Bandon and Cape Blanco Lighthouse. For an unusual whale-watching opportunity, take a flight from Aerial Photo and Sightseeing of North Bend, (541)756-2842.

Scenic Drive. South of Bandon, the landscape opens to reveal sparsely forested ocher hills dotted with thousands of grazing sheep. Heading out of town, a scenic alternative to the highway is Beach Loop Road (good for cycling). It parallels the ocean in view of a welter of sea-sculpted offshore rock formations, with evocative names such as Devil's Kitchen and Elephant Rock. The best known, Face Rock, is said to portray an Indian princess turned to stone by an evil spirit.

State Park Fun. Cape Blanco State Park (91814 Cape Blanco Rd; (541)332-6774), carved out of the 1,800-acre Hughes dairy ranch, covers most of the stormy cape. Its famous lighthouse, the oldest on the Oregon Coast, was built in 1870 and sits at the edge of the cape surrounded by grassy meadows— and miles of beautiful, uncrowded coastal scenery. The light remains active and can be seen 21 miles out to sea. Tours of the 59-foot-high tower are available April through October, Thursday

Sleep aboard an authentic stern-wheeler reproduction. The Na-So-Mah is the inspiration and creation of former home builder Joe Bolduc, who operates this floating inn year-round with his wife, Dixie. The River-boat B&B (moored on the Coquille River, (503)347-1922) remains moored at night and, weather permitting, casts off at 7:30am on a 2 1/2-hour cruise up the Coquille River during breakfast.

through Monday. Special evening tours of the lighthouse, complete with costumed guides and tall tales, are available by reservation from Siskiyou Coast Escapes of Port Orford; (541)332-2750. Although the areas around the lighthouse are closed to hikers, the 1,880-acre state park has an extensive trail network that leads from the headland down to beaches to the north and south, as well as a boat ramp on the Sixes River. The campground is set far enough back from the tip of the cape that the area's famous winds are bearable; it is open year-round and has RV, hiker/biker, and horse camps.

The historic Hughes House, down in the lowlands beside the Sixes River, was built in 1898 for $3,800 by R. J. Lindberg for the Hughes family. The two-story, 11-room cedar house, listed on the National Register of Historic Places, is a prime example of Eastlake Victorian architecture and is a curious anomaly out here on this isolated, rugged coast. Also within the park lie the eerie remnants of a cemetery and church, Mary, Star of the Sea, built by Patrick Hughes and once used by area settlers.

Hiking. One particularly special hike is out to Blackloc Point, where a stream plunges off a 150-foot cliff to the beach below. The easiest route to Blackloc Point (technically in Floras Lake State Park) is from Cape Blanco State Airport (yes, airport). The mile-long trail is managed by Cape Blanco State Park, (541)332-6774; call for directions.

RESTAURANTS

HARP'S   ★ ★

Don't expect unusual background music. The name comes from the presence of affable chef/owner Michael Harpster. Do expect a new, bigger, spectacular seafront location (just opening at press time). And do look for some wonderful halibut with hot pistachio sauce. Ditto for the grilled snapper, the pasta with prawns and a hot pepper and lemon sauce, and the charbroiled filet mignon marinated in garlic and teriyaki. Salads, a simple, enticing mix of homegrown greens, come with a tantalizing garlicky balsamic house dressing. Harpster also does a good job with his sweet onion soup made with beef broth and vermouth. Be sure to partake of the deep-fried mozzarella appetizers and the excellent wine list. *480 1st SW (½ block east of the harbor, in Old Town), Bandon, OR 97411; (541)347-9057; $$; full bar; AE, DIS, MC, V; checks OK; dinner every day.*

LORD BENNETT'S

 Occasionally, an oceanfront eatery with a killer view serves worthwhile food. Lord Bennett's is such a place; the saltwater vistas are stunning, and the sautéed and broiled shellfish selections are darn appetizing, also. In a break from pan-frying, oysters are poached, returned to their shells, and finished with mushrooms and mornay sauce, while snapper comes topped with an unusual walnut-garlic concoction. Jamaican jerked chicken (with pineapple salsa) and a vibrantly colored vegetable plate are other possibilities. Baked prawns with prosciutto, deep-fried calamari, and the French onion soup are first-rate appetizers. Weekends the place jumps with live bands downstairs. *1695 Beach Loop Dr (next to the Sunset Motel), Bandon, OR 97411; (541)347-3663; $$; full bar; AE, DIS, MC, V; checks OK; brunch Sun, lunch, dinner every day.*

LODGINGS

LIGHTHOUSE BED AND BREAKFAST ☆☆

 Spacious and appealing (although the groundskeeping is uninspired), this contemporary home has windows opening toward the Coquille River, its lighthouse, and the ocean, which is a short walk away. Guests can watch fishing boats, windsurfers, seals, and seabirds cavort in the saltwater surroundings. There are now five guest rooms (you can see the lighthouse from three), all roomy and wonderfully appointed. The Gray Whale Room, up on the third floor, is the real stunner, with a king-size bed, wood-burning stove, TV, and a whirlpool tub overlooking the three-sided, watery panoramas. Breakfasts are top notch, prepared by amiable hostess Shirley Chalupa. *650 Jetty Rd (at 1st St), Bandon; (541)347-9316; PO Box 24, Bandon, OR 97411; $$; MC, V; checks OK.*

"As far as we're concerned, California is just one big city—from Bakersfield to the Oregon border. Most of our customers are Californians.... The tourists are great. They're always in a good mood, never in a hurry, and they tell us where to go when we take a vacation."
—Martha Keller, owner, Misty Meadows

FLORAS LAKE HOUSE BED AND BREAKFAST ☆

 If the hot summer sun beckons you to cool swims in a freshwater lake, choose Floras. This modern two-story house offers four spacious rooms, each with a bath and deck access; two enjoy fireplaces. Most elegant are the North and South Rooms, but you can see Floras Lake and the ocean beyond from all four. Hiking and biking trails abound in this isolated area, and Floras Lake is great for windsurfers (and you might just have the beach to yourself). *92870 Boice Cope Rd (from Hwy 101, turn west on Floras Lake Loop, 9 miles north of Port Orford, and follow signs to Boice-Cope Park), Langlois, OR 97450; (541)348-2573; $$$; MC, V; checks OK.*

BANDON WAYSIDE MOTEL

This 10-unit, out-of-the-way motel occupies a parklike setting on the road to Coquille. Rooms (less than $35 in winter) are simple and clean, with an outdoor barbecue in the large backyard. Picnics are always a possibility, and the motel's quiet isolation, 2 miles from the beach, occasionally spares the visitor from the summer coastal fog. Housebroken pets are allowed at an extra charge. *1175 SE 2nd St, Bandon, OR 97411; (541)347-3421; $; AE, DIS, MC; no checks.*

SEA STAR HOSTEL AND GUEST HOUSE

Two lodgings in one, the Sea Star is a four-room guest house connected to a hostel by a diminutive courtyard. The guest house is considerably more lavish, so cheapsters should check into the men's and women's dorms. Here guests share bath, kitchen, dining room, laundry facilities, and a laid-back lounge (and help with the chores). Bunks are $16 a night (less for American Youth Hostel members and young kids); private rooms with shared baths go for about twice as much. The guest house features a natural-wood interior and harbor views. Skylights illuminate the two upstairs suites. In-room coffee and a TV are part of the package. *375 2nd St (take 2nd St off Hwy 101 into Old Town), Bandon, OR 97411; (541)347-9632; $$; MC, V; local checks only.*

SUNSET MOTEL

Everywhere along the coast, the closer you get to the ocean, the more expensive the rooms are. The Sunset is a worthwhile compromise. A clean, comfortable room with a limited view and a double bed is yours for about $50, while an oceanfront unit might be twice as much, or more. So opt for economy—you're just across Beach Loop Road from the ocean anyway, and the setting is unsurpassed. All rooms include a TV, use of a sizable indoor Jacuzzi, and morning coffee. *1755 Beach Loop Rd, Bandon; (541)347-2453 or (800)842-2407; PO Box 373, Bandon, OR 97411; $; AE, DIS, MC, V; checks OK.*

PORT ORFORD

Port Orford, the most westerly incorporated city in the continental United States, is also the rainiest place on the Oregon Coast. That doesn't bother most locals, who will tell you that what matters are its relaxed pace and terrific views. Oregon's oldest coastal town, Port Orford is far removed from big-city nuances, yet hip in its own way, especially considering the seasonal influx of board sailors and surfers, who head for Battle Rock and Hubbard's Creek beaches.

ACTIVITIES

Arts Festival. After commercial fishers and lumbermen, painters, weavers, sculptors, quilt makers, glassblowers, and other artisans make up a good portion of Port Orford's population of 1,100 or so. During the first week of May, the three-day Port Orford Arts Festival celebrates the visual and performing arts throughout the community. Galleries open their doors to all, the town hosts visual displays and performances, and craftspeople demonstrate their talents, all complemented by gourmet food booths. Call (541)332-0045 for details.

Humbug Mountain State Park. Towering darkly over the coast, mist-shrouded Humbug Mountain rises 1,750 feet above sea level. Humbug Mountain State Park campsites (open April through October) are located at the base of the massive headland, 6 miles south of Port Orford. A day-use area is three-quarters of a mile southeast of the campground entrance bordering Brush Creek. A scenic 3-mile path curves out of Brush Creek Canyon all the way up to the windblown peak. The Oregon Coast Trail also threads through Humbug Mountain State Park north from Rocky Point, passing the campground and emerging before the registration booth. On the way to the top, trailblazers encounter gigantic rhododendrons in bloom and eye-popping views of black-sand beaches and rocky, kelp-strewn shorelines. For complete trail information, contact Humbug Mountain State Park; (541)332-6774.

Ocean View. Don't miss the oceanside drive: Follow the Ocean View signs (painted with a huge arrow on the pavement), turning west from Hwy 101 on Ninth St, then south on Coast Guard Rd. Once over the little hill, you get a panoramic view of the harbor, Humbug Mountain, and Battle Rock—an off-shore promontory where in 1851 local Indians fought white settlers in one of the state's fiercest conflicts ever between Natives and whites. Stop at Port Orford Heads State Wayside for a picnic, and take a path leading to an expansive viewpoint encompassing Cape Blanco to the north and Humbug to the south.

Dinosaurs. There's no way you can miss the 25-foot-tall *Tyrannosaurus rex* standing out front, so you may as well pull over and have a closer look. No, it's not a leftover movie set from the *Flintstones*, but it does qualify as one of the Oregon Coast's certifiably wackier—albeit educational—attractions. The Prehistoric Gardens (36848 Hwy 101 S, Port Orford, OR 97465; (541)332-4463) are the brainchild of sculptor and self-taught paleontologist E. V. Nelson, who started creating life-size dinosaurs in 1953. Now, in addition to *T. rex*, there are another 22 mammoth models—including triceratops, pterodactyl, and stegosaurus—fashioned from steel and concrete and painted in unexpectedly bright hues. They're placed around the appropriately primeval setting of fern-choked rain forest, identified and explained by informative plaques. Younger kids especially will enjoy this. Admission: adults $5.50; children 12–18 $4.50, 5–11 $3.50. Open year-round every day. Yearly rainfall here can reach 10 feet, so complimentary umbrellas are provided.

LODGINGS

HOME BY THE SEA BED AND BREAKFAST   ☆

 The ocean view is one of southern Oregon's best, and you can see it from both guest rooms in this modest, homey B&B that sits atop a bluff near Battle Rock. There's easy beach access, and guests have the run of a large, pleasantly cluttered dining/living room area, also with an ocean view. Quiche, waffles, omelets, and fresh strawberries are the morning mainstays. You can surf the Internet with chatty Alan Mitchell, a friendly whirlwind of information and a Mac enthusiast. *444 Jackson St (1 block west of Hwy 101), Port Orford; (541)332-2855; PO Box*

606-B, Port Orford, OR 97465; alan@homebythesea.com; www.homebythesea.com; $$; MC, V; checks OK.

BATTLE ROCK MOTEL

Although this nothin'-fancy, retro-looking eight-room motel is on the wrong (east) side of Hwy 101, your fair-priced room is only a stone's throw from the cliffside trail of Battle Rock Wayside Park. Year-round whale watching and a wonderful stretch of uncrowded beach await. You're also within walking distance of most of Port Orford. *136 S 6th St, Port Orford; (541)332-7331; (PO Box 288), Port Orford, OR 97465; $; AE, DIS, MC, V; no checks.*

CASTAWAY BY THE SEA

 This 14-room motel sits atop a site formerly occupied by Fort Orford—the Oregon Coast's oldest military installation—and the Castaway Lodge, once frequented by Jack London. All rooms enjoy ocean views (the south-facing vistas of Humbug Mountain and beyond are stunning), and rates begin in the $40 range (even less in the off-season), remarkable for oceanfront lodgings. Suites—which sleep four to six and include kitchens, dining areas, and two bedrooms or a loft—are also reasonably priced. The beach, harbor, and shops are an easy stroll away. *545 W 5th (between Ocean and Harbor Drs), Port Orford; (541)332-4502; PO Box 844, Port Orford, OR 97465; $$; MC, V; local checks only.*

GOLD BEACH

For deep-sea fishing, check with Briggs Charters at the Port of Gold Beach, (503)247-7150, providing bait and tackle for four-hour excursions (July–September).

Named by 1850s miners for its once gold-laced sands, Gold Beach squeezes in snugly between the coastal headlands and the Pacific. The Rogue River—one of the dozen U.S. Wild and Scenic Rivers, renowned for its fabulous salmon and steelhead runs—divides Gold Beach from neighboring Wedderburn. Outdoorsman-author Zane Grey is numbered among the river's many admirers, and his writings helped bring the area to the world's attention.

ACTIVITIES

Angling Dreams. The stretch of the Rogue River between Gold Beach and Agness probably has more professional fishing guides than anywhere in Oregon. Gold Beach is an angler's heaven: Salmon, steelhead, cutthroat trout, and giant sturgeon swim the Rogue; snapper, cod, coho salmon, and perch are found offshore. Call the Gold Beach Visitors Center, (541)525-2334, for a listing of the guides, or contact the Rogue Outdoor Store (560 N Ellensburg Ave, Gold Beach, OR 97444; (541)247-7142), where you can also get fishing tips and rent tackle or clam shovels.

Rogue River Outfitters, (541)247-2684, offers a variety of fishing trips. The drift-fishing trip for fall steelhead includes equipment, lodging, food, and guide fees for $750 per person. A day-long fishing trip on the Rogue can be arranged any time of the year on the outfitter's covered boat. Fall steelhead are fished September to November; the bigger winter steelhead are caught January to early March.

River Trips on the Rogue. Just north of Gold Beach, Wedderburn is the home port of the Rogue River Mailboat, which has been mail carrier to folks upriver in Agness since 1895, when it was a two-day haul. Out of that necessary service has grown a busy recreational industry for several local operators, who whisk passengers on jet boat tours far into the scenic interior in just a couple of hours. River Rogue Mailboat Trips offers three different trips up the river to view harbor seals, ospreys, bald eagles, blue herons, black bear, black-tail deer, and other wildlife. The "Postage Due" trip is 64 miles long and takes you up to Agness. This is the gentlest ride and includes a two-hour meal break in Agness. The "Special Delivery" trip is 80 miles of white water through backcountry and includes a two-hour meal break in Agness. The "Handle With Care" is a 104-mile jet trip "up the down staircase" that is not for the faint of heart: You'll ride a 1,000-plus-horsepower hydro-jet as far upriver as the boat can go. For reservations or more information, call (800)458-3511, or stop by for same-day reservations at their dock on Rogue River Road; heading south, take the left before crossing the Patterson Bridge over the Rogue River. Another jet boat company offering three similar tours from the port of Gold Beach is Jerry's Rogue Jets; call (541)247-7601 for more information.

Whitewater raft traffic on the all-too-popular Wild and Scenic part of the Rogue is carefully controlled. River runners interested in unsupervised trips must sign up with the U.S. Forest Service, (541)479-3735, for a lottery during the first six weeks in the new year. Rogue River Outfitters, (541)247-2684, also offers guided white-water rafting tours.

Riverwalking. Trails cut deep into the Kalmiopsis Wilderness and Siskiyou National Forest, or you can follow the Rogue River. A jet boat will drop you off to explore all or part of the 40-mile-long Rogue River Trail along the north bank. Spring is the best time for a trek, before 90-degree heat makes the rock-face trail intolerable. Stay at any of seven remote lodges, where—for prices ranging from $55 to $180 per night—you end your day with a hot shower and dinner, and begin the next with breakfast and sack lunch. (Reservations are a must.) Rogue River Reservations dispenses information and can arrange booking on just about any Rogue River outing, jet boat trip, or overnight stay in the wilderness; (541)247-6504 or (800)525-2161.

Beachcombing. These days you'll find more agate and jasper than gold along the beaches outside of Gold Beach. Large trees and logs drift ashore, and storms deposit surf-washed agates, jasper, and the occasional fossil or Japanese glass float. The best beachcombing happens during the winter months, after a heavy storm. Go searching for agates and other semiprecious stones at low and high tides, when the waves churn the beach gravel, revealing nature's bounty.

Tide Pools. The Pistol River area (8 miles south of Gold Beach), Nesika Beach (7 miles north), and Rocky Point (25 miles north) beckon tide poolers with miniature sea life spread among the rocks and sand. Sea anemones, mollusks, sea urchins, starfish, and tiny hermit crabs dwell within each perfect ecosystem.

Oenophiles. The Whale of a Wine Festival, in mid-January or -February, takes place at the Curry County Fairgrounds in Gold Beach Saturday noon to 7pm, Sunday noon to 5pm. A $6 admission ticket buys you a souvenir wine glass and a chance to win door prizes. Inside, sample Oregon's finest wines, dine at local restaurant food booths, watch seminars on whale migration, check out the art show, buy some arts and crafts, and sample gourmet coffees. Contact the Gold Beach Visitors Center for information; (800)525-2334

Short and Sweet. Cape Sebastian State Park lies at the end of a steep road, accessed via Hwy 101, 6 miles south of Gold Beach. From there you have a choice of two viewpoints, one to the north and another to the south. Cape Lookout is on the northern horizon, 43 miles away, and California's Point St. George can be seen to the south, 50 miles away. The 1,104-acre park has a 2.5-mile trail that drops 720 feet in elevation south to the beach at Meyers Creek. Open from sunup to sundown.

End of the Oregon Coast Trail. Cape Ferrelo and Lone Ranch Beach, both near milepost 352, mark the southern end of the designated route of the Oregon Coast Trail. The 250-foot-high cape, a good spot to fly a kite, is connected by a 1.5-mile trail north to the House Rock viewpoint. Lone Ranch Beach is a popular spot for tide-pool exploration and beachcombing.

Horseback Riding. Indian Creek Trail Rides, (541)247-7704, leads tours of the coastal mountains with abundant opportunities to see wildlife. The stable is located on the south bank of the Rogue River east of Gold Beach on the Lower Rogue River Hwy. Hawk's Rest Ranch, (541)247-6423, has rides on the beach, through the dunes, and on the ranch's land at Pistol River. Located up North Bank Rd from the Pistol River Store,

"Why do I like living in Gold Beach? If my car breaks down on the side of the road, I know I'll know the guy who's going to stop and help me."
—Wendy Lang, lifelong resident of Gold Beach

the ranch is family owned and operated. Sunset rides on the beach are a highlight.

RESTAURANTS

THE CAPTAIN'S TABLE ☆

 This funky-looking structure overlooking the highway (with nice ocean views, too) is Gold Beach's old favorite. Nothing is breaded or deep-fried, so a broiled salmon or halibut is a good choice (although doneness is not always consistent). The corn-fed beef from Kansas City is meat you can't often get on the coast. Scallop-and-beef kabobs (with bacon, bell peppers, and onions) are interesting choices. The dining area, furnished with antiques, is moderately small and can get smoky from the popular bar. The staff is courteous, enthusiastic, and speedy. *1295 S Ellensburg Ave (on Hwy 101, south end of town), Gold Beach, OR 97444; (541)247-6308; $$; full bar; MC, V; local checks only; dinner every day.*

NOR'WESTER ☆

From the windows of the Nor'Wester you may watch fishermen delivering your meal: local sole, snapper, halibut, lingcod, and salmon. Most seafood is correctly cooked (broiled or sautéed), and served garnished with almonds or some other simple topping. Forgo the more complicated, saucy preparations (such as the snapper Florentine). You can also find a decent steak, or chicken with Dijon or orange glaze (and a cranberry-apple relish). The fish 'n' chips are tasty and the clam chowder respectable. *Port of Gold Beach (on the waterfront), Gold Beach, OR 97444; (541)247-2333; $$; full bar; AE, MC, V; checks OK; dinner every day.*

LODGINGS

INN AT NESIKA BEACH ☆☆☆

 Is this secluded inn, located in residential Nesika Beach, the Oregon Coast's finest B&B? Many visitors to the three-story neo-Victorian (built in 1991) think so. A jewel of a structure occupying a bluff overlooking the ocean, the inn boasts lovely landscaping, a relaxing wraparound porch, and, in the back, an enclosed oceanfront deck. The expansive interior, with exposed hardwood floors and attractive area rugs, is grandly decorated. All four guest rooms are upstairs, and all four enjoy fabulous ocean views, uncommonly comfortable (and large) feather beds, and private baths with spas. The third floor annex with its fireplace and bay window overlooking the Pacific offers the ultimate night's stay. Hostess Ann Arsenault serves a full breakfast (in a dining room facing the ocean) that might include crêpes, scones, egg dishes, and muffins. *33026 Nesika Rd (west off Hwy 101, 5 miles north of Gold Beach), Gold Beach, OR 97444; (541)247-6434; $$$; no credit cards; checks OK.*

TU TU'TUN LODGE ☆☆☆

The lodge complex, named after a local Indian tribe, is one of the loveliest on the coast, though it's 7 miles inland. Tall, mist-cloudy trees line the north shore of the Rogue River, and hosts Dirk and Laurie Van Zante will help you get a line in for salmon or steelhead (or for trout in the spring-stocked pond a mile upriver). The main building is handsomely designed, with lots of windows and such niceties as private porches overlooking the river, racks to hold fishing gear, and stylish, rustic decor throughout. There are 16 units in the two-story main building and two larger kitchen suites in the adjacent lodge, all with river views. In the apple orchard sits the lovely Garden House, which sleeps six and features a large stone fireplace. The nearby two-bedroom and two-bath River House is the spendiest and most luxurious, with a cedar-vaulted living room, outdoor spa, satellite TV, and washer/dryer. All guests can swim in the heated lap pool, use the four-hole pitch-and-putt course, play horseshoes, relax around the mammoth rock fireplace in the main lodge, hike, or fish. A sweet-smelling, madrona-wood fire is lit every evening on the river-view terrace, and you might spot the two resident bald eagles anytime. Breakfast, hors d'oeuvres, and a prix-fixe dinner are served

The Rogue River Jet Boat Marathon in mid-June kicks off with "Calcutta" on Friday night, the big to-do before the race—everyone's welcome. On Saturday, the racers take off from Jot's Resort (on the estuary, north side of the bridge; (800)367-5687) and go up to Agness; spectators gather at Jot's for the grand finale.

(for an additional $37.50 per person). The four-course evening meal might include your own fish as the entree, or perhaps chicken breasts with a champagne sauce, or prime rib. Outside guests can dine here also (by reservation only). *96550 N Bank Rogue (follow the Rogue River from the bridge up the north bank for 7 miles), Gold Beach, OR 97444; (541)247-6664; $$$; full bar; MC, V; checks OK; breakfast, dinner daily (restaurant open May–Oct only).*

JOT'S RESORT

 The manicured grounds of this rambling resort spread along the north bank of the Rogue River, adjacent to the historic Rogue River Bridge and just across the river from the lights of Gold Beach. The 140 rooms, all with water vistas, are spacious and tastefully decorated, and many have refrigerators. If you just want a standard room, ask for one of the newer ones ($85). The two-bedroom condos ($155), with kitchens, accommodate six. There's an indoor and outdoor pool, spa, and weight room; rent a boat to explore the riverfront. Rogue River jet boats and guided fishing trips leave right from the resort's docks. And, of course, all the necessary angling gear can be rented. *94360 Wedderburn Loop (at the Rogue River Bridge), Gold Beach; (541)247-6676 or (800)367-5687; PO Box J, Gold Beach, OR 97444; $$; AE, DC, MC, V; checks OK.*

GOLD BEACH RESORT

 Stay here for in-town beachfront accommodations. This sprawling complex is close enough to the ocean that roaring surf drowns out the highway noise. All the rooms and condos have private decks and ocean views. There's an indoor pool and spa, and a private, beach-access trail leads over the dunes to the ocean. The roomy condos come with fireplaces and kitchens. *1330 S Ellensburg (Hwy 101, near south end of town), Gold Beach, OR 97444; (541)247-7066 or (800)541-0947; $$; AE, DC, MC, V; no checks.*

BROOKINGS

Just 6 miles north of the border, in the heart of what's known as the Banana Belt for its mild year-round climate, Brookings is a booming retirement community for Oregonians and Californians. But more than retirees thrive in the warm winter and early spring; lilies (90 percent of the U.S. supply) and azaleas grow en masse in maintained gardens.

With one of the safest harbors on all the Oregon Coast, Brookings is also a busy port town. The contemporary sprawl has obscured some of Brookings's original character, but the coast is as gorgeous as ever, bookending the town with scenes of breathtaking beauty. To the northwest are the Samuel H. Boardman and Harris Beach State Parks; to the east are the verdant Siskiyou Mountains, deeply cut by the Chetco and Winchuck Rivers.

ACTIVITIES

Wildlife Viewing. To find nature's elusive creatures, charter a boat from the harbor to watch the gray whale migration in January or spy the pods from one of the vantage points along the highway. Capes Sebastian and Ferrelo and Harris Beach State Park are designated whale-watching sites. In late February, squawking Aleutian Canada geese gather at Lake Earl at the mouth of the Smith River. Goat Island, at 21 acres the largest offshore island in Oregon, was the first to be protected in the Oregon Islands National Wildlife Refuge system. Located offshore from Harris Beach State Park, the island has nesting colonies of puffins, auklets, guillemots, murres, gulls, cormorants, and storm-petrels. Other area birds include spotted owls, marbled murrelets, bald eagles, ospreys, and red-tailed hawks.

From the Pioneer Days. Chetco Valley Historical Museum (Museum Rd, (541)469-6651), the oldest standing structure in the area, is a former way station and trading post. Dating back to 1857, the wooden home contains much of what you'd expect—a spinning wheel and several old sewing machines, a trunk from 1706, photographs depicting the harbor area's rich history, Native American artifacts, a hoary moonshine still—and the exceptional: an iron casting of a face, which some believe to be the image of Queen Elizabeth I, perhaps left behind in

Brookings is promoting eco-tourism these days in order to keep its visiting whales and geese, frolicking elk, black bear, sea lions, and steadfast redwoods from disappearing. If you have a penchant for preservation, the Chamber of Commerce would be happy to accommodate you: choose from tide pool cleanup, erosion control, and habitat improvement; (800)535-9468.

the 1500s by Sir Francis Drake. Open from mid-March to November. Free.

Flower Fest. As a center for flower growing, Brookings celebrates an annual Azalea Festival on Memorial Day weekend. But for fresh flowers year-round, look for the sign to Flora Pacifica's viewing garden and flower mart (15447 Ocean View Dr; (541)469-9741 or (800)877-9741), south of town. Many of their creations incorporate wild greens responsibly harvested from the surrounding woodlands. Wreaths made from all-natural materials are also for sale. Hydrangeas, statice, artemesias, pennyroyal, salal, myrtle, as well as herbs grow in the farm's maintained gardens.

Smoked from the Sea. The Great American Smokehouse and Seafood Company (15657 Hwy 101; (541)469-6903 or (800)828-FISH) has Indian-style smoked salmon jerky strips, smoked tuna and jerky, lox, and a variety of other seafood, smoked and fresh. No doubt about it, at $25 per pound the salmon jerky is pricey, but so good. Smoky, rich, and peppery, it's worth the couple of bucks for a Magic Marker–size stick to nosh on. The place prides itself on dolphin-free products, hook-and-line fishing, and absolute freshness. They ship anywhere.

Historic Trail. The Bombsite Trail, 18 miles east of Brookings, is highly recommended by locals. Located on Forest Service Rd #1205 after spur #260 (take South Bank Rd to Mt. Emily Rd), it is 1 mile long and meanders through an old-growth redwood forest. At the end is the site that was hit by two Japanese incendiary bombs during World War II. Fifty years later, the pilot, Nubuo Fujita, visited Brookings and donated his family's 400-year-old samurai sword to the city as a gesture of "trans-Pacific amity."

Redwood and Myrtlewoods. The Brookings-Harbor region contains the greatest diversity of conifers in the world, among them redwoods, Brewer spruce, myrtlewood (which grows only on the southern Oregon Coast and in Palestine), and plants associated with serpentine soils. Alfred A. Loeb State Park offers inland campsites near Brookings, 10 miles up Chetco River Rd. The 320-acre riverside park sits amid an old-growth grove of myrtlewood trees surrounded by redwoods. The park's Riverview Trail connects to the Siskiyou National Forest's Redwood Nature Trail, where trees are as old as 800 years, to create a lovely 2-mile loop. The largest redwood is 286 feet tall with a circumference of 33 feet.

In front of the historical museum is the largest Monterey cypress in the United States.

Brookings in Bloom. Azalea State Park, north of downtown Brookings, is best known for its gorgeous blooms in May and for the Azalea Festival, held here on Memorial Day weekend. Recently the 36-acre park added a fantasyland playground, with turrets, slides, and wooden skyways that smaller kids will love. Take the short path up to the gazebo to fully survey the landscaped grounds, or sit at one of the handmade myrtlewood picnic tables to watch the butterflies (plentiful in early summer) flit from flower to flower.

Tent With a View. Just 1 mile north of Brookings, fearless and friendly gulls mind Harris Beach State Park, which has overnight camping (151 sites) and day-use facilities in addition to great wraparound views. A seascape painter's dream, the park's driftwood coastline is dotted with gnarled basalt outcroppings with such descriptive names as Hunchback and Whales Head.

Samuel H. Boardman State Park. Strung out over 11 miles of coastline, Samuel H. Boardman State Park has numerous day-use waysides. The 1,471-acre park begins at Burnt Hill Creek, 2.5 miles south of the mouth of the Pistol River, and extends to within 4 miles of Brookings (from mile posts 341 to 352). Picnic areas are located at Arch Rock, Whalehead Cove, and Lone Ranch Beach at Cape Ferrelo, all marked along the highway. Each has outstanding views of the rugged coastline, plus access to beaches and the Oregon Coast Trail. The park has many short trails that lead from highway pullouts to scenic viewpoints: The Natural Bridges Cove viewpoint along Hwy 101 has a paved walkway at the south end of the lot that leads through fern, fir, old-growth spruce, and alder to a monumental overlook of crashing surf and rock archways. Indian Sands Trail at milepost 349.2 leads half a mile through a wooded area to a sand dune cliff. Whalehead Cove is the largest day-use facility in the park at milepost 349. A rock formation in the cove resembles the shape of a whale's head, complete with a blowhole

Brookings, only 4.8 miles from the California border, has one of the better networks of bike lanes of any of the coastal cities.

that spouts water when the waves hit it just right. Also, don't miss where the Oregon Coast Hwy crosses Thomas Creek Bridge near milepost 348; at 345 feet above the creek, the bridge is the highest in Oregon.

RESTAURANTS

CHIVES ★

Here's a place that has the town talking: a top-drawer eatery unceremoniously stuck into a Hwy 101 strip mall. Disregard the setting; inside, the mood's casual but upscale. Both the lunch and dinner menus offer lots of variety, including preparations previously unknown on the south coast. For example, veal is as rare in Brookings as a winter freeze, but Chives purveys a classic *osso buco*— although it's served with garlic mashed potatoes rather than the traditional risotto. A creamy wild-mushroom risotto accompanies the roast duck, and a rock-shrimp risotto appetizer can be had. *1025 Chetco Ave (north end of town, along the main drag), Brookings, OR 97415; (541)469-4121; $$; full bar; MC, V; checks OK; brunch Sun, lunch, dinner Wed–Sun (closed in Jan).*

HOG WILD CAFE ★

A pig theme runs rampant here: pig dolls, pig cups, and all manner of swinelike paraphernalia. The food is worth pigging out on, too. You'll find jambalaya, Cajun meatloaf, a prime rib sandwich, and a veggie lasagna and frittata. The "kitchen sink" pasta comes with andouille sausage, snapper, shrimp, and scallops in a zesty marinara sauce. Great breakfasts with pig-size muffins, and coffee drinks that sport names such as Hog Heaven (chocolate-coconut mocha). *16158 Hwy 101 S (west side of Hwy 101, 1 mile south of Brookings-Harbor bridge), Harbor, OR 97415; (541)469-8869; $; beer and wine; AE, DIS, MC, V; local checks only; breakfast, lunch every day.*

RUBIO'S

This gaudy-yellow restaurant along the Hwy 101 strip is your best bet for south coast Tex-Mex. The chiles rellenos and the chile verde are top-notch choices, and the salsa is outstanding (it's available by the bottle if you need to take some on the road). For something different, try the Seafood à la Rubio, a dish combining fresh lingcod and shellfish in a jalapeño-stoked garlic and wine sauce. *1136 Chetco Ave, Brookings, OR 97415; (541)469-4919; $; full bar; AE, DIS, MC, V; checks OK; lunch, dinner Tues-Sat.*

LODGINGS

CHETCO RIVER INN   ☆☆

Expect a culture shock: This secluded, alternative-energy retreat sits on 35 forested acres of a peninsula formed by a sharp bend in the turquoise Chetco River, 17 miles east of Brookings (pavement ends after 14 miles). Isolation isn't a problem, because there are no phones, except for innkeeper Sandra Brugger's cellular phone. The place is not so remote that you can't read by safety propane lights and watch TV via satellite (there's even a VCR). The large, open main floor—done in a lovely, deep-green marble finish—offers views of the river, myrtlewood groves, and wildlife. A full breakfast is included, and Sandra will pack a deluxe sack lunch or serve an exemplary five-course dinner on request. Fishermen and crack-of-dawn hikers (the Kalmiopsis Wilderness is close by) are served early-riser breakfasts. All told, this is getting away from it all without roughing it. *21202 High Prairie Rd (follow North Bank Rd 16 miles east, left after South Fork Bridge, take second guest driveway on left), Brookings, OR 97415; (541)670-1645 or (800)327-2688 (Pelican Bay Travel); $$; MC, V; checks OK.*

SOUTH COAST INN   ☆☆

Twin gargoyles guard this handsome, 4,000-square-foot, Craftsman-style home designed in 1917 by renowned San Francisco architect Bernard Maybeck. It's situated two blocks above downtown, so traffic noise is audible, but the structure—one of the city's oldest—is surrounded by sound-proofing trees and shrubs, some of them flowering all year in the mild Brookings climate. A spacious, partially covered

Discover Oregon of Brookings, (800)924-9491, offers guided, interpreted mountain-bike tours on forest roads and easy trails in Siskiyou National Forest along the coast. Trips last from a few hours to several days and include bike rentals and meals.

Soak up the Chetco
harbor ambience,
and scarf an order
of halibut 'n' chips
at Pelican Bay
Seafoods, 16403
Lower Harbor Rd,
(541)469-7971.

deck, lighted in the evening, extends around most of the house. Three guest rooms (two with ocean views) are luxuriously appointed with myriad antiques. The downstairs parlor sports a stone fireplace and a grand piano, while a workout room includes a weight machine, sauna, and hot tub. An unattached cottage (with bedroom and kitchen) lacks the house's charm. Innkeepers Ken Raith and Keith Popper will even pick you up at the nearby Crescent City (California) airport. No children under 12 or pets. *516 Redwood St (turn east on Oak St, north on Redwood, 2 blocks above Hwy 101), Brookings, OR 97415; (541)469-5557 or (800)525-9273; scoastin@wave.net; www.virtualcities.com; $$; AE, DIS, MC, V; checks OK.*

HOLMES SEA COVE BED AND BREAKFAST ☆

Jack and Lorene Holmes offer two guest rooms on the lower level of their cozy ocean-view home north of town (as well as a connected, private guest cottage with a living-room nook, refrigerator, and private deck). The home sits on a waterfront bluff, with a trail that winds its way down to the ocean and to a private park with picnic tables. Lorene brings a continental breakfast to your room. *17350 Holmes Dr (take Hwy 101 north to Dawson Rd, left to Holmes Dr), Brookings, OR 97415; (541)469-3025; $$; MC, V; checks OK.*

BEACHFRONT INN

If you want an oceanfront motel room in Brookings, this Best Western right at the mouth of the Chetco River is the closest you can get. Every one of the hundred or so units is beachfront and enjoys a private balcony. Some are a mere 100 feet away from breaking surf. Microwaves and refrigerators, a heated pool, and an outdoor spa are all part of the deal. The fishing and pleasure-boat fleet moors next door. *16008 Boat Basin Rd (off Lower Harbor Rd, south of the Port of Brookings), Brookings; (541)469-7779 or (800)468-4081; PO Box 2729, Harbor, OR 97415; $$; AE, DC, MC, V; checks OK.*

SEA DREAMER INN BED AND BREAKFAST

 Hugs, cookies, and a friendly dog's affection can be had at this 1912 country Victorian built from local redwood. Backed by evergreens and located south of town and just a half mile from the ocean, the home looks out over ever-blooming flowers, fruit trees, and lily fields, which slope gently to beach level. There are but three rooms, two with shared bath and all enjoying Pacific vistas. The splendid interior includes a piano, a fireplace, and a formally decorated dining area where full breakfasts are served. Kids and most pets okay, as long as both are well behaved. *15167 McVay Lane, Brookings, OR 97415; (541)469-6629 or (800)408-4367; $; no credit cards; checks OK.*

INDEX

BEST PLACES®
DESTINATIONS
OREGON COAST
REPORT FORM

Based on my personal experience, I wish to nominate the following restaurant or place of lodging; or confirm/correct/disagree with the current review.

_____

_____

_____

_____

(Please include address and telephone number of establishment, if convenient.)

REPORT

Please describe food, service, style, comfort, value, date of visit, and other aspects of your experience; continue on another piece of paper if necessary.

_____

_____

_____

_____

_____

_____

_____

_____

I am not concerned, directly or indirectly, with the management or ownership of this establishment.

_____
SIGNED

_____
ADDRESS

_____

_____
PHONE   DATE

Please address to Best Places Destinations and send to:

SASQUATCH BOOKS
615 Second Avenue, Suite 260
Seattle, WA 98104
Feel free to email feedback as well: books@sasquatchbooks.com

BEST PLACES®
DESTINATIONS
OREGON COAST
REPORT FORM

Based on my personal experience, I wish to nominate the following restaurant or place of lodging; or confirm/correct/disagree with the current review.

_____

_____

_____

_____

(Please include address and telephone number of establishment, if convenient.)

REPORT

Please describe food, service, style, comfort, value, date of visit, and other aspects of your experience; continue on another piece of paper if necessary.

_____

_____

_____

_____

_____

_____

_____

I am not concerned, directly or indirectly, with the management or ownership of this establishment.

_____
SIGNED

_____
ADDRESS

_____

_____
PHONE   DATE

Please address to Best Places Destinations and send to:

SASQUATCH BOOKS
615 Second Avenue, Suite 260
Seattle, WA 98104
Feel free to email feedback as well: books@sasquatchbooks.com